PLACE NAMES OF THE WELSH BORDERLANDS

by

Anthony Lias

'What this mountain means, and the dark valley, and the field full of folk, I shall show you clearly'.
- William Langland, *Piers Plowman* (1377)

For Pat

Published by
Palmers Press, 5 Castle Street, Ludlow
and Printed by
Orphans Press Ltd., Hereford Road, Leominster.

ISBN 1 870054 04 0

CONTENTS

LIST OF MAPS

ABBREVIATIONS

Bd	Bedfordshire	La	Lancashire	We	Westmoreland
Bk	Buckinghamshire	Le	Leicestershire	Wo	Worcestershire
Brk	Berkshire	Li	Lincolnshire	YE	East Riding of Yorkshire
Ca	Cambridgeshire	Mx	Middlesex		
Chs	Cheshire	Nb	Northumberland	YN	North Riding of Yorkshire
Co	Cornwall	Nf	Norfolk		
Cu	Cumberland	Np	Northamptonshire	YW	West Riding of Yorkshire
D	Devon	Nt	Nottinghamshire		
Db	Derbyshire	O	Oxfordshire	Gw	Gwent
Do	Dorset	Ru	Rutland	Pow	Powys
Du	Durham	Sa	Shropshire (Salop)		
Ess	Essex	Sf	Suffolk	Br	Breton
Gl	Gloucestershire	So	Somerset	Corn	Cornish
Ha	Hampshire	Sr	Surrey	OE	Old English
He	Herefordshire	St	Staffordshire	W.	Welsh
Hrt	Hertfordshire	Sx	Sussex		
Hu	Huntingdonshire	W	Wiltshire	cp.	compare
K	Kent	Wa	Warwickshire	c.	*circa*, approximately

A NOTE ON THE WELSH COUNTIES

POWYS	old Breconshire, W. Brycheiniog (Sir Frycheiniog)
	old Montgomeryshire, W. Trefaldwyn (Sir Drefaldwyn)
	old Radnorshire, W. Maesyfed (Sir Faesyfed)
GWENT	old Monmouthshire, W. Sir Fynwy, from R. Mynwy (Monnow)
CLWYD	old Denbighshire, W. Dinbych (Sir Ddinbych)
	old Flintshire, W. Fflint (Sir Fflint)
DYFED	old Pembrokeshire, W. Penfro (Sir Benfro)
	old Carmarthenshire, W. Caerfyrddin (Sir Gaerfyrddin)
	old Cardiganshire, W. Ceredigion (Sir Aberteifi)
GWYNEDD	old Caernarvonshire, W. Caernarfon (Sir Gaernarfon)
	old Merionethshire, W. Meirionydd (Sir Feirionydd)
GLAMORGAN	(same) W. Morgannwg (Sir Forgannwg)
(LLOEGR	the Welsh name for England)

INTRODUCTION

This short handbook is intended for the use of anyone wishing to find out a little more about the place names of the Welsh Borderlands region and the contribution they can make towards a richer understanding of the historical landscape.

The author feels there may be a genuine need for such a book, since although - obviously - a great amount of work extending over a great many years has been carried out in the place-name field generally, detailed surveys such as those contained in the County volumes of the English Place-Name Society do not really cater for the needs of non-specialists. In the Borderlands, too, the question of Welsh names has to be considered, and more than 200 of these are dealt with in the pages that follow.

The aim throughout has been to stimulate as well as to inform without placing undue burdens upon the reader. And while it was clearly impossible to deal with every single location, the cross-section provided has been designed to show what handy guides place names can turn out to be - not only to geology and geography but also to the people influenced by these ever-present factors. Fortifications, burial places, boundaries, ways of making a living, money and moneyers, trade routes, beliefs and superstitions, fiscal matters, law: all these are among the things reflected in names found on both sides of the Border.

Hence the names themselves are not treated according to any alphabetical or geographical plan; instead, they take their natural place in the narrative wherever they illustrate a particular topic - boundaries, say, or money. However, they are listed alphabetically in the index.

A reminder may be useful here. To get at the meaning of any place name it is almost always necessary to know something about its older form or forms, since the modern ones tend to be at best misleading or at worst meaningless. The linguistic reasons for this hard fact of life are touched on only sparingly in the present book, but they help to explain why (for example) LUDLOW was written *Ludelawa* in a revenue return of 1177.

So that the reader may see at a glance the varying degrees of change, each first mention of a place following Chapter 1 is usually followed by at least one older form, placed in brackets. Very often the oldest form available comes from Domesday Book - e.g. BADGER Sa (*Beghesovre* DB). In certain cases where still older forms exist, at least one of these is supplied first if relevant - e.g. WROXETER Sa (*Ouirokónion* c. 150, *Rochecestre* DB). In other cases again, only a post-Domesday form is supplied; and this is either because there is no adequate entry in the great survey of 1086 - as with Ludlow - or because the later form proves more useful in context, as with FOWNHOPE He (*Faghehop* 1242). The value of this method will quickly become apparent.

Chapter 1 provides a brief guide to the historical background against which the names of the region have developed; something is said here, too, about the languages involved - since some readers may be a trifle hazy about who spoke or wrote what, and in which period. (It should also be noted that the Old English letter *đ* is equivalent to *th.*)

As a matter of convenience, the abbreviations used in respect of English counties follow those found in Eilert Ekwall's *Dictionary of English Place-Names* (4th ed., 1960); the much larger debt to the *Dictionary* itself must also be acknowledged.

Wherever applicable, the spellings of Welsh place names are based on *A Gazetteer of Welsh Place-Names* (Cardiff, 1957); in other cases the relevant Ordnance Survey maps have been consulted, and in general the translations are of the forms printed in one or other of these sources.

H. D. G. Foxall's *Shropshire Field-Names* (Shrewsbury, 1980) was an invaluable help in the writing of Chapter 7, as were the series of documents and maps concerning Shropshire parishes prepared by the Local Studies Library in Shrewsbury under the Community Programme contract with the Manpower Services Commission. With regard to these publications, and to the many others consulted by the author, any errors of fact or interpretation lie firmly at his own door.

CHAPTER 1

PLACE NAMES *ARE* HISTORY

When the Roman conquest of Britain began in 43 AD the whole of what is now Shropshire, together with most of Herefordshire and part of Cheshire, was in the hands of the tribe the Romans called *Cornovii*. To the south-west of them lay the territory of the *Silures* (in modern Gwent), while to the south-east were the *Dobunni* (in Gloucestershire). The Powys of today was held by the *Ordovices*.

Between them, then, these tribes controlled the region bounded by Dee, Severn and Wye familiar to us under the name 'Welsh Borderlands'. ('Welsh', as will be seen later, is simply a word used by the Anglo-Saxons to mean 'foreign', 'Celtic', 'British'.) It seems likely that they had started settling here somewhere around 300 BC, if not before; by that time, the Iron Age in Europe was well into its second phase and immigrants from the seaboard of Gaul (modern France and Belgium) were busy spreading the Iron culture to our shores.

Exactly how the tribes just mentioned gained ascendancy is far from clear. But, like their kinsmen elsewhere in Britain, they must presumably have edged out or absorbed earlier Iron and Bronze Age settlers - using existing hillforts and creating new ones of their own as political, economic and cultural centres. The traveller in the Borderlands cannot go far without encountering impressive examples of these structures.

The language spoken - *British* - was the forerunner of Welsh, Cornish, and the Breton of Brittany. In some areas, too, there may have been speakers of the early forms of Irish Gaelic (Goidelic) - which, with Gaulish, made up the other great branches of Celtic.

Cornish, like Gaulish, has now virtually died out. But the other branches live vigorously on, much of their vocabulary having weathered long centuries of change. Even in their ancient forms, not all Celtic words still in use would be entirely unrecognisable; and scores of those connected with enduring features of life and sustenance - answering to words like *timber, cow, curds, milk, hide, fleece, flax, corn, leaven, malt, honey, mead, iron, ingot, coal, hearth* and so on - were as alive and well in Roman times as they are today. This is a very worthwhile point to remember.

The Romans themselves recorded a good number of Celtic tribal and place names in Britain, and writers such as Caesar provide interesting insights into the ways in which they were fitted into the formal structure of the Latin tongue. To these writers, and to the Roman administrators, we owe the bulk of the earliest place-name material for the country as a whole.

Clearly, many of these place names must have belonged first of all to hillforts, and then been transferred to the Roman forts or towns which replaced them. In the Borderlands, Roman Wroxeter in Shropshire probably replaced the hillfort on the Wrekin (see Chapter 2); in Herefordshire, the forts at Leintwardine *(Bravonium, Bravonio)* and Buckton Park may have replaced any or all three of the earlier settlements at Croft Ambrey, Coxall Knoll and Brandon Camp; still in Herefordshire, the town at Kenchester *(Magnis)* probably replaced the massive hillfort at Credenhill; in Gwent, Caerwent *(Venta)* may have borne the same sort of relationship to the enclosure at Llanmelin. Just outside our area proper, the original Roman fort at Cirencester *(Corinium)* was sited near to the Celtic 'oppidum' at Bagendon, which even possessed its own mint.

Place names, then, reflect continuity as well as change. But the story by no means ends there. The Anglo-Saxons had still to come; and *their* place-namings, in turn, were influenced in a great many cases by what had been left ready to hand by their Roman and Romano-Celtic predecessors. Indeed, it would be very surprising if the Cornovii, Silures and other Celtic settlers did not themselves owe something to still older lore surviving from the Bronze Age.

Going back to the various sites mentioned above, all of them are on or close to Roman roads. These, obviously, must have served commercial and economic as well as military purposes. The road from Wroxeter to Leintwardine ran past Linley and the Stiperstones - a prize source of lead (from which silver could be obtained) and copper. The road from Kenchester ran past Sutton Walls hillfort (near Hereford), where iron-working may have taken place, and on to Gloucester *(Glevum);* and this road, like the one from Hereford to Monmouth *(Blestium, Blestio),* catered for the Forest of Dean - rich in coal as well as iron - and its outlets on Wye and Severn.

Yet another road from Kenchester was aimed towards Abergavenny *(Gobannium, Gobannio),* which also boasted ironworkings; while to the north, the stretch of Watling Street from Wroxeter to Chester *(Deva)* and beyond homed on the lead of Cheshire and the copper of North Wales and Anglesey *(Mona).* Again strictly out of our area, but still of interest, the fort at Car-

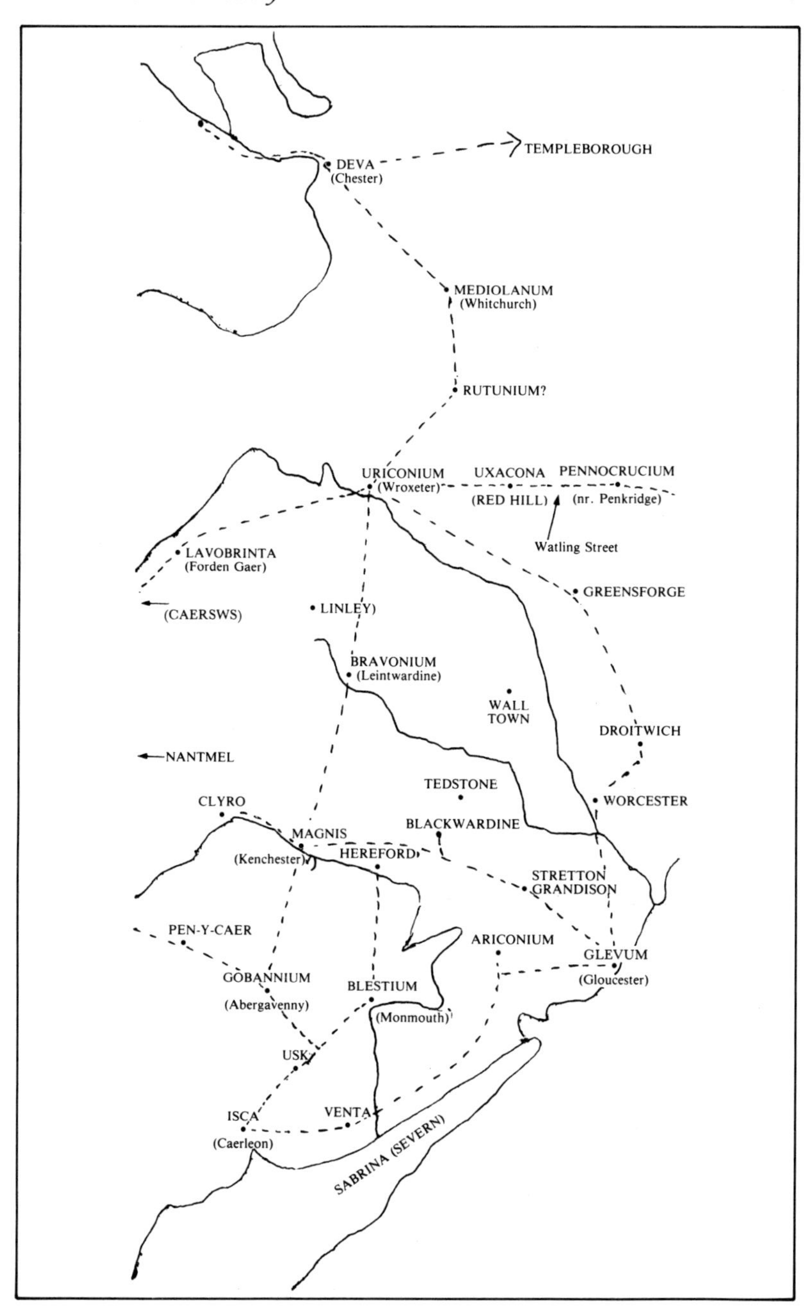

ROMAN ROADS, FORTS AND TOWNS
IN THE BORDERLANDS

marthen probably had relevance to the gold deposits in the territory of the *Demetae;* for the Romans certainly mined gold at Dolaucothi, near Pumsaint.

The ever-practical Romans, therefore, had good reasons for being in the Borderlands - indeed, as Caesar makes clear between the lines *(Gallic War),* their conquest of Britain had a lot to do in the first place with the country's reputed wealth and trading links.

By 410 AD the legions had gone, and the Roman administration was no longer effective. But the 350 years or so of their occupation had added greatly to the wealth and trade just mentioned. Britain was as attractive a prospect to the marauding Anglo-Saxons, who had already made many piratical raids on its coasts, as it had been for the Romans. From roughly 449 AD onwards they began to arrive in ever-increasing numbers.

The Anglo-Saxons were a Germanic people, speaking the language now usually known as Old English. (Almost all the Old English words which appear in our place names have close relatives in German, Scandinavian or Dutch.) It took them upwards of 150 years to gain the upper hand in Britain; and in some instances they must have come to agreements with the British tribes rather than resorting to violent solutions.

The story of this latest settlement is unfolded in the terse year-by-year entries of the *Anglo-Saxon Chronicle,* which ranks with Domesday Book both as a priceless source of information and as a formidable achievement in its own right. Kept going in several different centres by many different hands, it outlasted not only the struggles between Saxon and Briton and - later - those between Saxon and Viking, but also (remarkably) the Norman Conquest itself, for the final entry was not made until 1154.

From around 449 right up to 1066, place-name endings like *-ham, -ingham, -stead, -stow, -stock, -ton, -ington, -don, -ingdon, -hill, -bury* and *-well,* among many others of Old English type, must have crept into use in more and more parts of the country as the Anglo-Saxons settled down. The early years of the 9th century saw the Vikings beginning to add their characteristic *-thorpe,* * *-brigg* and *-rigg* endings - especially, though not exclusively, in the north and east. (As already mentioned, the Vikings 'shared' some place-name words with the Anglo-Saxons, whose language was not so vastly different from their own; though - to take one typical example - BEOBRIDGE in Shropshire might well have taken the form BEOBRIGG in the north or east, since the Old English 'soft' *g* was 'hard' in Scandinavian.)

* The equivalent OE word usually gave the place-name ending *-throp.*

A quick glance at a map suffices to show that most place-name endings of the Old English type are represented throughout the Borderlands - purely Celtic names also occur, of course - and that *-thorpe, -brigg, -rigg* are in short supply. As we shall see, these endings tell us various interesting things. At the same time, the *beginnings* of names ('first elements') tend to be rather more ambiguous: and this adds further spice to the whole subject.

The importance of seeing the early forms of names (see Introduction) is well illustrated by the case of ATCHAM, Shropshire. This is the spelling found on maps and signposts, and it has its own - somewhat unusual - history in terms of pronunciation. But its *meaning* can only be got at through the Domesday spelling *Atingeham* - to which is owed the 'learned' version of the name found in ATTINGHAM PARK. ATCHAM was in fact originally named after a person of some importance (see Chapter 6).

The French-speaking Norman conquerors of 1066, whose scribes were responsible for the Domesday entries, seem to have left well alone in the matter of place-naming itself: they were content to record what they actually heard and saw. New French coinings are rare indeed - though personal or family names like Lacy, Bagot, Burnell, Carbonel, Harcourt, Drew (from *Dru* or *Drogo*), Beauchamp and so on often came to be added to others already established - e.g. ASHFORD CARBONEL, near Ludlow. Even names which *appear* new - e.g. GROSMONT, Gwent, 'Large hill' - may sometimes be straightforward translations of older forms lost to us, for bilingual or even multilingual clerks must surely have existed.

It remains only to mention the Latin which occasionally occurs in early entries, or which survives on the map in forms like MAGNA, 'great', 'large', PARVA, 'small', IUXTA, 'near, next to', etc. This is almost always due, not directly to the Romans, but to monks who wrote in Latin as a matter of course. Men like these, who had been present in Britain from the times of the earliest conversions, were often very learned and had access to all sorts of written material. As for the Church in general, its later power and influence is obviously shown in names like BISHOPS CASTLE and PRIORS HALTON (Shropshire), MONKLAND (Herefordshire), and a great many others of the same type.

To sum up:- The place-names of the Borderlands reflect patterns of change and continuity which go back to a very ancient date and which are paralleled elsewhere in Britain. If this brief guide helps readers to find their way around more easily in time as well as space, it will have served its purpose adequately.

CHAPTER 2

THE HAND OF MAN

THE WREKIN, looming up in eerie fashion from its surrounding plain, could justifiably be taken as the focal point of Shropshire if not of the entire Borderlands region. There is a well-known Shropshire toast, 'to friends around the Wrekin', and it is easy enough to believe that it enshrines an ancient tradition.

If the hillfort straddling this great ridge was in reality the tribal centre of the Cornovii before the Romans overcame them, then it seems more than probable that its name was transferred to Roman WROXETER. The earliest forms of this *(Ouirokónion, Viroconium, Uriconium)* were all recorded c. 150-300 AD and may contain the known Gaulish personal name *Virico* - though it is worth noting that there was also a tribe *Viro*mandui in Gaul as well as a fort *Viro*sidum in northern Britain.

When the Romans quitted Wroxeter (c. 90 AD), they handed the place over to the Cornovii as their official capital. And if history had taken a slightly different course, there might have been a county called WREKINSET to add to Dorset and Somerset - both of which names were formed with the help of Old English *sǣte,* 'settlers', 'inhabitants'. The Anglo-Saxons actually used a phrase *Wreocensǣte,* 'settlers near the Wrekin', but its further development was not to be.

For in the event, neither Wroxeter nor the Wrekin managed to retain more than nominal importance. Following their advance into the region (around the beginning of the 7th century), the interest of the English warlords seems to have shifted to SHREWSBURY - a rather involved place name, this, but one which needs explanation for the precise reason that it, rather than the Wrekin, accounts for the name SHROPSHIRE.

The site of Shrewsbury began life as the Celtic PENGWERN - which, as Gerald of Wales tells us, can mean 'Head of the Alder-grove' (as well as 'End of the Swamp', an alternative modern interpretation). By 901 it had been renamed *civitas Scrobbensis,* 'Scrob-city'; in 1006 we find *Scropesbyri,* and in 1016 *Scrobbesbyrig* - 'fortified place of (the) Scrob'. Who - or what - Scrobb was remains unclear; but by 1006 the name itself was sufficiently well-established to merit the use of the wider term *Scrobbesbyrigscir,* 'shire with the fortified place of (the) Scrobb as its head'. Domesday has *Sciropesberie* for the town, *Sciropescira* for the shire; the latter, or perhaps the *Scrobscyr* of 1087, gave SHROPSHIRE. Another Norman-French form, *Salopescira,* gave SALOP.

The differing pronunciations Shr*ow*sbury and Shr*oo*sbury do not really concern us here. However, it is interesting that Shropshire folk are still heard to say that they are 'going to Salop' when the town, Shrewsbury, is meant; a relic, possibly, of long-forgotten French influence.

Going back for a moment to WREKINSET, this is by no means as fanciful as it might seem. A *Chronicle* entry for the year 1016 refers to the *Scrobsǣte,* 'settlers near (the) Scrob' - so again, it is only a matter of chance that SHROPSHIRE was initially preferred to SCROBSET or SCROBSETSHIRE.

We have just seen how the focus of power shifted from the Celtic Wrekin to Roman Wroxeter and then to English Shrewsbury. But even here - witness PENGWERN - the English would have had first to dislodge Celtic defenders.* What happened to these Celts and to others like them? It is not known for certain; but there can be no question of wholesale massacres amounting to genocide (as used once to be imagined). In most cases, once the decisive battles were over, the British will have continued to live peaceably side by side with the English.

Names like WALCOT Sa (*Walecota* 1160), near Wellington, WALTON Chs (*Waletona* 1154-60) and WALLASEY Chs (*Walea* DB), WALFORD He (*Walecford* DB), and WALSWORTH Gl (*Waleswurthe* 1221), all testify to this fact - as do WELSH HAMPTON Sa and WELSH NEWTON He, though these are late namings.

The key elements here are OE *walh* (plural *walas*), 'foreigner', 'Celt', and *welisc, welsc,* 'foreign', 'Celtic'. According to Caesar, one of the first Celtic tribes encountered by the Germans were the *Volcae* - or a branch of them - and it is probable that this tribal name was the source of OE *walh* in its double sense. (In colloquial German, *welsch* means 'foreign' to this day.)† Naturally enough, when the Germanic Anglo-Saxons reached these shores they applied the term *walas* to the British Celts as well, occasionally using the combined form *Bret-walas*.

Since this book is specifically concerned with the Welsh Borderlands, including parts of Wales, it is important to stress

* Who may even have had names like *Cadfael*, which appears to mean something like 'Battle-iron'.

† Similarly, in Irish speech, *Gall* meant both 'a Gaul' and 'a foreigner (in general)'.

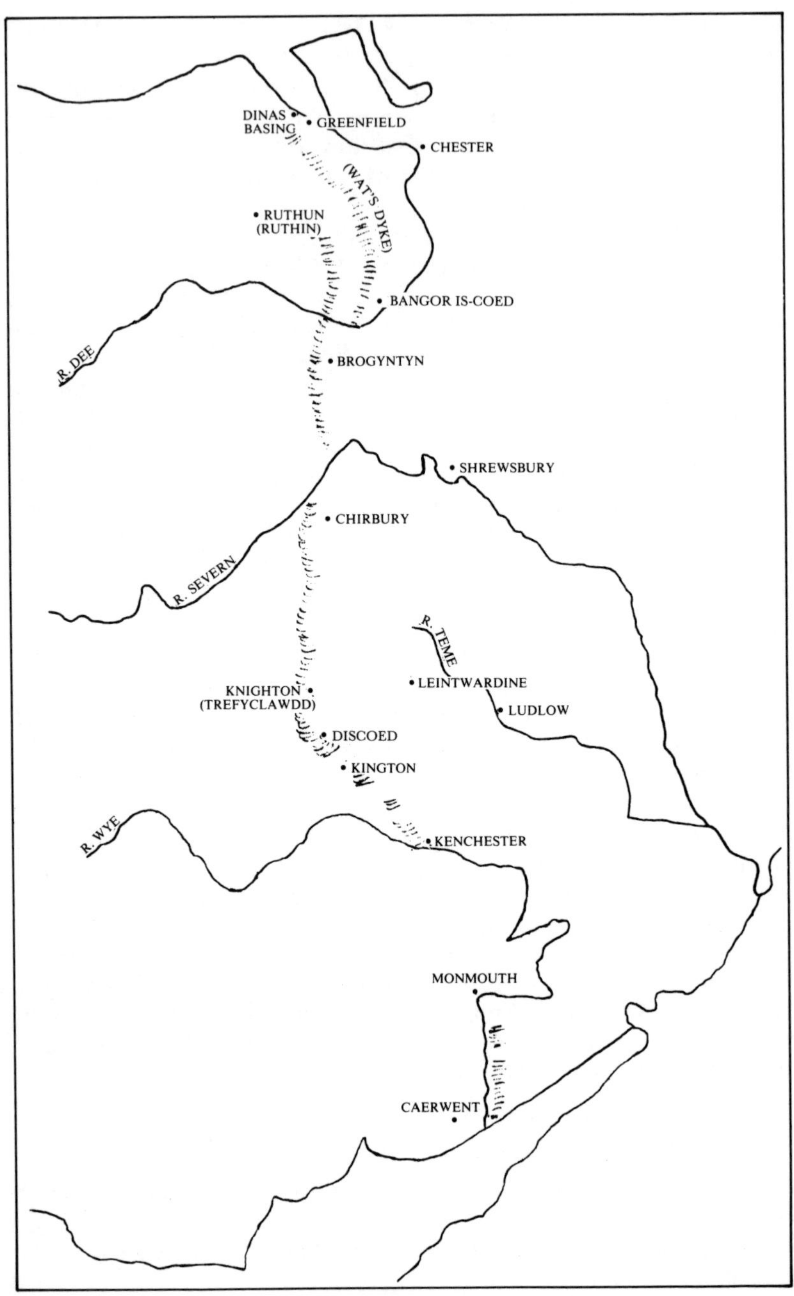
DINAS
BASING
GREENFIELD
CHESTER
(WAT'S DYKE)
RUTHUN
(RUTHIN)
BANGOR IS-COED
R. DEE
BROGYNTYN
SHREWSBURY
CHIRBURY
R. SEVERN
R. TEME
LEINTWARDINE
KNIGHTON
(TREFYCLAWDD)
LUDLOW
DISCOED
KINGTON
R. WYE
KENCHESTER
MONMOUTH
CAERWENT

OFFA'S DYKE

that the name WALES itself represents OE *Walas,* 'Foreigners', 'Celts', just as WELSH represents OE *welsc*, 'foreign', 'Celtic'. Strictly speaking, the English conquerors might have used the word WALES, i.e. *Walas*, to described the whole of mainland Britain south of the Forth; no contradiction would have been involved. The name BRITAIN, Latin *Britannia,* prevailed in this context only because it echoed still older terms for both country and people found by the Romans.

As for our Welsh neighbours, they once referred to themselves in a generalised way as *Brythoniaid*, 'Britons'; but, when English conquests finally separated them from their kinsmen elsewhere, they adopted the narrower term *Combroges*, 'fellow-countrymen', which in time became *Cymry*. When, therefore, we see the word 'Welsh' used in books about place names, it is perhaps helpful to see it in this wider context.

One final word is necessary about OE *walh.* Because some Celts in Britain were enslaved by the Saxons, and because a proportion of Celts and Saxons alike drifted down to 'serf' status later on, *walh* came to mean 'slave' as well as 'Celt', 'Briton', 'Welshman'. But cases where this meaning applies in place names are not easy to detect.

We saw above that Shrewsbury came to lend its name to a whole shire (OE *scīr*) or county (old French *counte*). The same sort of process took place with CHESTER, whose earliest name *(Dēoua, Deva)* means 'goddess' and refers to the river DEE. By c.730 the town was called *Legacaestir* in OE, 'Fort of the legions', *Carlegion* in Welsh (same meaning). By the time of Domesday Book these names had been abbreviated to OE *Cestre*, '(at the) fort, walled city'. Already by 980, we find *Legaceasterscir* for the county, and the DB *Cestrescire* gave CHESHIRE, i.e. CHESTER-SHIRE.

MONMOUTH - Roman BLESTIUM, BLESTIO - is *Monemude* DB '(town at) the mouth of the Monnow'. The Welsh form *Mynwy* for the river gives TREFYNWY for the place -'Town on the Mynwy', W. *m* changing to *f* after *tre*, *tref* (we shall see various other examples of this sort of change as we go along). MONMOUTHSHIRE (W. MYNWY or SIR FYNWY) is now of course GWENT, reflecting the element *Venta* in the old *Venta Silurum* (CAERWENT, site of a flourishing Roman town).

HEREFORD (same in DB) seems to mean 'Army-ford', the first element being OE *here*, 'army', also 'Danish army'; but it is worth mentioning that the Welsh name for the town, HENFFORDD, signifies 'Old Road, Track'. Hereford had its first bishop before the end of the 7th century, and by 1038 we find HEREFORDSCIR for the county.

MONTGOMERY Pow perpetuates the name of Earl Roger de Montgomery, who held the first Norman castle built here soon after the Conquest in order to overawe the Welsh. The Welsh name for the place, TREFALDWYN, means 'Town of Baldwyn' - he was a Lieutenant of the Marches - and here we see that W. *b* also changes to *f* after the feminine noun *tre(f)*. The nearby hillfort, FRIDD FALDWYN, would appear to echo the later town-name.

KNIGHTON Pow signifies 'Tūn of the knights or men-at-arms' (OE *cniht*). In this instance the Welsh name, TREF-Y-CLAWDD or TREF-Y-CLO, 'Town on the dyke', refers to Offa's Dyke, the great earthwork built by the Mercian King Offa (757-96), which was the fore-runner of the present English-Welsh border and which passes through Knighton.

The name POWYS is thought to be derived either indirectly from Latin *pagus*, 'province', 'district', or directly from a Welsh word *powys*, 'rest', 'repose', 'pause' (this word occurs in old dictionaries of the Welsh language and may be compared with Corn. *powes* and Br. *paouez*, which have the same meanings). Powys was brought under the sway of the Mercian English in the early 9th century.

Knighton might well have been called DITCHTON, DYKETON, or the like (cp. DITCHFORD Wo, WANSDYKE Ha, etc.), since OE *dīc*, 'ditch', 'dyke', 'embankment' is an element frequently used in place names referring to earthworks of various kinds. More usually the reference is to pre-English constructions; and the same applies to OE *weall*, 'wall', 'rampart' (from Latin *vallum*), to OE *ceaster*, 'fort', 'walled city' (from Latin *castrum*, 'fort', *castra*, 'camp'), and - to a lesser extent - to OE *burh*, *byrig*, 'defended place'.

In the Borderlands, comparatively few places which are still inhabited have names showing the first three OE elements mentioned above, though they are quite common throughout the country as a whole. DIGLEY Chs (*Dyghleg* 1287) may contain *dīc*; DIXTON Gl (*Dichelesdona* 1175) may contain a personal name, *Diccel,* derived from it. WALL St (*Walla* 1167) is an obvious *weall* candidate, since it is taken to be the site of the Roman station of LETOCETO - the source of the name LICHFIELD (*Liccidfeld* c.730). Joining Chester and Wroxeter (*Rochecestre* DB) in the *ceaster* category are KENCHESTER He (*Chenecestre* DB), CHESTERFIELD St (*Cestrefeld* 1167) - Roman remains have been found at the second place - CHESTERTON Gl (*Cestertone* DB), CHESTERTON Wa (*Cestretune* 1043) - there was a Roman fort near here - and WOODCHESTER Gl (*Wuduceaster* 896), also a Roman site.

OE *burh* and *byrig* occur very much more frequently, and some of the inhabited places whose names contain one or other of these elements will be listed in a moment. First, though, it will be useful to look at them alongside *dīc*, *weall* and *ceaster* in the context of uninhabited *prehistoric* sites - since these, obviously, are among the chief attractions of the Borderlands.

OE *burh* gives modern *burg(h), borough, burrow* and *brough*; its 'inflected' form, *byrig*, gives *berry* and the widely distributed - if sometimes confusing - *bury*. In both cases, the 'correct' meaning is that of 'defended place'; but it is human to err, and in later Old English and in Middle English (c.1100-1500) *burh* and *byrig* tended to be confused with *beorg* (see the subject of *burial*, below).

With regard to prehistoric fortification, we see our keywords in action at BURY DITCHES Sa, near Bishop's Castle (hillfort); BURY WALLS Sa, near Weston-under-Redcastle (hillfort; Weston itself has been suggested as the site of Roman RUTUNIUM); THE DITCHES Sa, near Shipton (hillfort); BURY BANK St, near Stone (hillfort); BURROW CAMP Sa, near Hopesay (hillfort); SUTTON WALLS He, near Sutton St. Nicholas (hillfort); ACONBURY HILL He, near Kingsthorne (hillfort); RISBURY CAMP He, near Humber (fort); ULEY BURY Gl, near Uley (hillfort); CASTLE DITCH Chs, near Delamere (hillfort, on EDDISBURY HILL); and THE WALLS Sa, near CHESTERTON - one case where a *ceaster* name may refer direct to a hillfort rather than to a Roman site.

As might be expected, the term *burh* (or *byrig*) was also used by the Anglo-Saxons to denote their own defended sites. Even so, it is accepted that most inhabited places where the term occurs are likely to owe their 'name-status' to the nearby presence - or suspected presence - of older fortifications.

With this proviso, place names in Shropshire derived from *burh* in one or other of its forms include:- ALBERBURY, BECKBURY, BROUGHTON, BURFORD, BURLEY, BURLTON (near a hillfort), BURTON, CHIRBURY, CLEOBURY MORTIMER (site of a Roman fort), CLUNBURY (near Bury Ditches), DIDDLEBURY, HORBURY, LYDBURY NORTH (an ancient manor), MAESBURY, NORBURY, PONTESBURY (near a hillfort), RUSHBURY (probably the site of a fort), SIDBURY and THORNBURY.

Herefordshire has ACONBURY (near a hillfort), AVENBURY, BURGHILL, BURLTON, BURRINGTON, GLASBURY, RISBURY (near a fort), SAWBURY and THORNBURY. In Cheshire are BREDBURY, BUNBURY, BURLEYDAM, HENBURY, MARBURY, NORBURY, PRESTBURY, WRENBURY and WYBUNBURY. Gloucestershire has ALMONDSBURY, MAUGERSBURY, PENBURY, PRESTBURY, SODBURY and THORNBURY. (Needless to say, places showing OE *burh* or *byrig* are very much less thick on the ground in Powys and Gwent, where English colonisation was patchy.)

Some of the names mentioned above will be met with again later under different headings. But we certainly ought not to leave the topic of defended sites without a look at the Welsh words most often found in this context - *caer, din, dinas, castell.* And THE BERTH, an intriguing name found both in Shropshire (near Baschurch) and in Staffordshire (near Maer), may prove to have something useful to tell us about Welsh survivals in place namings generally.

W. *caer* signifies both 'city' and 'fort'; it is of Celtic origin and not a borrowed form of Latin *castra.* We saw it used to denote CHESTER (*Carlegion* c.730, later *Caerlleon*), and it was similarly used for CAERWENT (*Cair Guent* c.800, *Cairguent* c.1150), a Roman city; in the case of CAERLEON-ON-USK Gw, W. CAERLLEON-AR-WYSG, the place was originally named after the river itself, *Isca*, to give *Iskalis* (for Isca legionum, 'Isca of the legions'), c.150, then *Cair Legeion guar Usic*, 'City of the legion(s) on the Usk', c.800.

CAERSŴS Pow was also a Roman site, as were Y GAER Pow (at Forden, Roman LAVOBRINTA) and Y GAER Pow (near Builth Wells) - both these last two meaning simply 'The fort' (W. *c* in the feminine noun *caer* becomes *g* after the definite article). Pre-Roman sites denoted by *caer* include CAER CARADOC Sa, 'Fort of Caratacus', CAER EINON Pow, 'Fort of Einon', CAER DU Pow, 'Black fort', GAER FAWR Pow, 'Great Fort' (here the definite article has been lost before *caer*) and TWYN-Y-GAER Gw, 'Hillock of the fort'.

CAERNARVON is obviously outside our area, but it provides an excellent example of continuity. Here the Romans built the fort of SEGONTIUM in the territory of the *Segontiaci*; either this fort or a predecessor was later named *Caer Seiont*, 'Fort of Segontium or the Segontiaci', and then CAERNARVON, 'Fort in Arfon' (an ancient cantref of Gwynedd). The stones of the

Roman fort were used in the building of the great 13th-century castle - which, like the word *caer* itself, is still going strong.

As for THE BERTH Sa, St, we noticed in the two Y GAER names above that initial W. *c* in a feminine noun becomes *g* after the definite article - *caer*, but *y gaer*. Now W. *perth*, which is also feminine, means 'thornbush', 'brake', and after the definite article the *p* changes to *b*, giving *y berth*, 'the thornbush'. It is quite possible, therefore, that THE BERTH is a direct semi-translation of W. Y BERTH, and the interested reader will find more evidence to support this particular suggestion in Chapter 8. In general, however, it ought to be said here that the chances of Welsh influence in Borderlands place names are always fairly strong.

W. *din*, from a British word *dūno-*, means 'fort'. It is rare in the Borderlands, but may occur in DINEDOR He (*Dunre* DB, *Dinra* 1170), where there is certainly a hillfort. But the DB entry may consist of OE *dūn*, 'hill', plus W. *bre*, which has the same meaning and would therefore make this a bi-lingual name (cp. BREDON Wo, where the same two words have been combined in reverse order). DINMORE He (*Dunemore* 1189, *Dinemor* 1273) appears to lack a hillfort; this name may be OE *dūn* plus W. *mawr*, 'great', and either 'Great hill' or 'Great (potential) fort' seems possible.

W. *dinas*, 'fort', 'city', is a related word found in DINAS BRÂN, Clwyd (near Llangollen), 'Fort of Bran', 'Fort of the Raven', and in several other names in Wales beyond the Borderlands. It is far less common than *castell*, 'fort', 'castle' (from Latin *castellum*), which is also used more flexibly. At CASTELL DINAS Gw, near Talgarth, *castell* denotes a Norman motte built inside a prehistoric fort (*dinas*); while at CEFN-Y-CASTELL Pow, near Middletown, the meaning is 'Ridge of the fort' - and here the fort (*castell*) is itself prehistoric. At CASTELL COLLEN Pow, near Llandrindod Wells, 'Hazel fort'*, the fort was a Roman one. (DINAS BRÂN, Clwyd, is also known as CASTELL DINAS BRÂN, on account of the medieval castle here.)

But it is time to move on to the subject of *burial*, which occupied so important a place in the minds of our distant forebears. Burial mounds or tumuli are as thick on the ground as hillforts and other fortified sites, and have given rise to any number of legends and superstitions everywhere. The vast majority of such mounds are pre-Celtic (neither Celts nor Romans favoured this type of burial), while a few belong to the period of Anglo-Saxon

* There was also a 7th-century saint named Collen.

paganism lasting until not much later than about 650 AD. Nevertheless in this field too there are 'keywords' in both Welsh and Old English.

The two words most often used in OE to denote burial mounds or tumuli were *hlāw* (which survives as *low*) and *beorg* (which survives as *barrow* or *berrow*). Both words, however, were also used of natural hills or mounds as well as burial mounds - the only sure way of deciding which sense was intended being physical investigation.

Thus MUTLOW Chs (*Motlow* 1354) refers to an assembly - *gemōt* - mound, and not to a known burial mound as such. BROMSBERROW Gl (*Bromesberga* c.1180) seems to mean no more than 'broomy hill', whereas BRIGHTWELLSBARROW in the same county refers to a burial mound proper.

To add to this tricky problem, *beorg* was frequently confused with OE *bearu*, 'grove', and also with *burh, byrig* (see above). Thus BARROW Sa (*Barwe* 1267) means 'grove', not 'barrow' in the sense of 'burial mound' - and the same applies to BARROW Gl. There are, too, modern *borough* and *bury* names - which ought to denote fortifications - whose meaning is that of 'mound' or 'hill', as indicated by their early forms, e.g. MODBURY Do (*Motberge* 1265), another assembly-mound. (Such cases as these show the importance of the early forms themselves.)

Thankfully, all is not lost. Names in *low* are rather more common in our area than names in *barrow* or *berrow*, and they do not present quite the same complexities. Most are derived fairly regularly from *hlāw*, which appears as *lawe, laue* or *lawa* in early entries.

An excellent example of a *low* name involving burial is LUDLOW Sa. The place was already known as *Ludelaue* in 1138, on account of a large mound on the east side of the (then) church, now St. Laurence's. In 1199 the mound was demolished so that the church could be enlarged - bringing to light three sets of bones. Even at that early date, then, excavation was capable of proving its value in confirming the reasons behind place-namings. (As for the bones, the clergy displayed them as belonging to three convenient Irish saints, making a steady income from the offerings of visitors.)

Other interesting *low* names in the region include LONGSLOW (*Wlonkeslawe* 1242), MUNSLOW (*Munsselawe* 1256), ONSLOW (*Andreslav* DB), PEPLOW (*Pippalawe* 1256), PURSLOW (*Pusselawe* 1226-8) and WHITTINGSLOW (*Witokeslawe* 1208) - all in Shropshire - and WOLFERLOW

(*Wulfereslow* 1242) in Herefordshire. It is conjectured that these names may commemorate the (pre-Christian) mound burials of seven Anglian warlords - Wlanc, Mundel, Andhere, Pyppa, Pussa, Hwittuc and Wulfhere respectively. OFFLOW St (near Lichfield), 'Offa's tumulus', may fall into the same category.

For TWEMLOW Chs (*Tuamlawe, Twamlawe, Tuamlowe* beside *Twemelawe* in early entries), it is worth noting that Gaelic *tuam* means 'sepulchre', 'tomb'. (This name is usually taken to represent OE *be twǣm hlāwum,* 'by two hills or tumuli').

Noted in the margin of a 12th-century transcript of the Hereford Domesday is the name *Hundeslawe*, 'Hill or grave of Hund (or of the hound)'. This place is now lost, but had the name survived its natural development would probably have given us another HOUNSLOW to add to the one (*Hundeslauwe* 1242) in Middlesex.

Welsh terms commonly used in connexion with burial mounds or cairns include *carn* (plural *carnau*), *carnedd* (plural *carneddi, carneddau*), and *bedd* (plural *beddau*). But a word of warning is required, since only *bedd* consistently has the meaning 'grave', 'sepulchre' in site-names; *carn* sometimes signifies 'hill or mountain with a fort' - effectively, 'hillfort' - while *carnedd* can mean simply 'mountain'. A good archaeological handbook is the best guide here. (The occurrence of forms such as Y GARN, GARN, Y GARNEDD, GARNEDD is again due to the W. definite article, which changes initial *c* to *g* in these words even though it may disappear itself.)

Among *bedd*-type names are BEDD ILLTUD Pow (near Penpont), 'Grave of Illtud' (a 6th-century saint of Breton origin), BEDD Y CAWR Pow (near Llanymynech), 'Grave of the Giant', and perhaps BESLOW Sa. This latter name is taken to be 'Betti's *hlāw*', but there are good grounds for thinking that *Beteslawe* DB and *Beszelawe* 1176 may contain W. *bedd* (or Br. *bez*, same meaning). BESLOW - with TWEMLOW - may qualify as a 'bilingual' name of the BREDON type.

W. *crug* is very like OE *beorg* and *hlāw* in that it means (hill(ock)', 'mound' as well as 'tumulus', 'cairn'. Also, it is like W. *carn* in that it may be used in the context of a hill crowned by a fort - e.g. CRUG HYWEL Pow (near Llanbedr), 'Mound or Fort of Hywel'. The diminutive form CRUGYN is found near Rhayader Pow, where the meaning is 'Little cairn'.

Old W. *crūc* (from *crouc-*) originally passed unchanged into OE as *crūc*. It is identifiable in CREECH BARROW Do (hill) and CREECHBARROW HILL So (*Crycbeorh* 682), and is thought to be the source likewise of a variety of names containing *crich, crick, crook, cruck, crutch* and *crouch*. However, some of these names raise questions worthy of further discussion (see Chapter 8).

The Borderlands are rich in fortified sites of all kinds, rather less so in burial mounds; they are a significant part of man's contributions to the landscape. But what of the landscape itself - literally, 'shape of the land' (OE *sceapan*, 'shape', 'create')? Here, too, place names have a wide variety of interesting things to tell us.

CHAPTER 3

THE HAND OF NATURE

A great many place names are of the type known as 'topographical' - that is, they make statements about various aspects of the environment, including contours, rock-formations, soil-types, springs and rivers, trees, plants, birds, animals and so on. Sometimes these statements are framed in a very general way - e.g. RUDGE Sa (*Rugge* DB), which is simply OE *hrycg*, 'ridge'; sometimes they are rather more specific, e.g. BROMLOW Sa (*Bromlawe* 1255), OE *brōm* plus *hlāw*, 'Broom hill'; and sometimes they are more specific still, e.g. STRETFORD He (*Stratford* DB), OE *strǣt* plus *ford*, 'Ford where a (Roman) road crossed a river'.

On the whole, topographical names tend to be reasonably informative: we are told *something* useful about a place or area. And in this respect, Celtic names are no more or less vague than their English counterparts. One very early example from Roman Britain, MARGIDUNUM or MARGIDUNO (near Nottingham), is taken to mean 'Marly fort' (Br. *marg,* Latin *marga,* 'marl') - a fairly precise description if correct; while, in the Borderlands as in Wales at large, Welsh names may also range from the general - e.g. CEFN, 'Ridge' (various places) - through the more specific - e.g. CEFN BRITH Pow, 'Speckled ridge' - to the more specific still - e.g. CEFNPYLLAUDUON Gw, 'Ridge of the black pits (or pools)'.

To some extent topographical names are a direct response to the environment, prompted by the simple human need to 'feel at home'. At the same time, others must reflect the equal need to survive by turning nature to advantage - i.e., they overlap with the type of name dealt with in Chapter 4. We shall see what is meant by this a little later on.

Names which state a bare minimum about the environment include Romano-Celtic MEDIOLANUM, MEDIOLANO (now Whitchurch, Sa), 'Middle-of-the-plain', and UXACONA (Red Hill, Sa), 'High (hill)'. Among later names in this category are HEATH Sa (*La Hethe* 1267), which is self-explanatory here; CLIVE Sa (*Cliva* 1176), 'Cliff'; EDGE Sa, Chs, Gl, 'Edge', 'Ridge' (OE *ecg*); (LONG) MYND Sa, MYNDE He, 'Mountain' (W. *mynydd* - most purely Welsh *mynydd* names have some descriptive addition); MERE Chs, 'Lake' (OE *mere*); RUDGE Sa, mentioned above; LITH Gl, 'Slope' (OE *hlið*); KNOCKIN

Sa (*Cnukin* 1196), 'Small rounded hill' (W. *cnycyn,* from *cnwc*); THE GOGGIN Sa, near Ludlow, probably W. (Y) GOGAN, 'Convexity', 'Hump'; CLEE Sa (*Clivas* 1232), 'Cliffs', designating the hills themselves - the irregular form CLEE here being due, seemingly, to the early forms of other regular CLEE names in the vicinity (see below); BREN Sa, W. *bryn,* 'hill'; RHYN Sa, W. *rhŷn,* 'hill'; CRUG Pow, near Knighton, 'Hill'; FRON Pow, near Knighton, probably W. (Y) FRON, 'The Hill', from *bron;* DEAN Gl, 'Valley' (OE *denu*); HOPE Sa, near Shelve, 'Valley' (OE *hop*); and OVER Chs, Gl, 'Slope', 'Ridge' (OE *ofer*).

The above examples are obviously not exhaustive, but in fact names of this 'simplex' type are comparatively uncommon. It is more normal to find words like *ecg, clif, denu, hop, bryn* etc. combined with other words so as to give 'compounds' - and these serve either to extend the range of topographical meaning or to indicate the presence of settlements in given topographical settings.

Thus we find topographical terms combined with adjectives - e.g. BRADLEY Sa, Gl, St, 'Broad *lēah* or stretch of open land' - or with nouns, e.g. WOODBATCH Sa, probably 'Valley with a wood'; but names of this type add little to our understanding. In the same way, EDGETON Sa, Chs, Gl, 'Village on a ridge', OVERTON Sa, Chs, 'Village on a slope', and HOPTON Sa, He (there are several HOPTONs in Shropshire) 'Village in a valley', are examples of settlement-names; but they do not tell us very much. In the present chapter, we shall be concerned with names, both English and Welsh, containing topographical elements from which definite facts can be gleaned (and perhaps other facts inferred). Sometimes settlements are involved, sometimes not.

Among birds featuring in Borderlands names the eagle (OE *earn,* W. *eryr*) is prominent. EARNSTREY Sa (*Ernestreu* 1172) is 'Eagle's tree', while EARNWOOD Sa (*Erne Wode* 1327), ARELEY Wo (*Erneleia* c. 1138) and ARLEY Wo (*Earnleie* 996) all mean 'Eagle wood'. CRUG ERYR Pow, near Llanfihangel Nant Melan, is 'Eagle hill'. OE *hafoc* is found in Hawkstone Sa (*Hauekestan* 1185), 'Hawk's stone' - and there is plenty of evidence to show that falconry was well-established in Anglo-Saxon England.

OE *cran,* 'crane', 'heron', appears in CRANMERE Sa, 'Crane lake or mere' and CRANHAM Gl, 'Cranes' *hamm* or water-meadow'. CRANAGE Chs (*Craulach* c. 1247) is 'Crow stream' (OE *crāwe, crāwan*), while the W. *brân* already seen in DINAS BRÂN occurs in CARREG-Y-FRÂN Pow (near Garth-

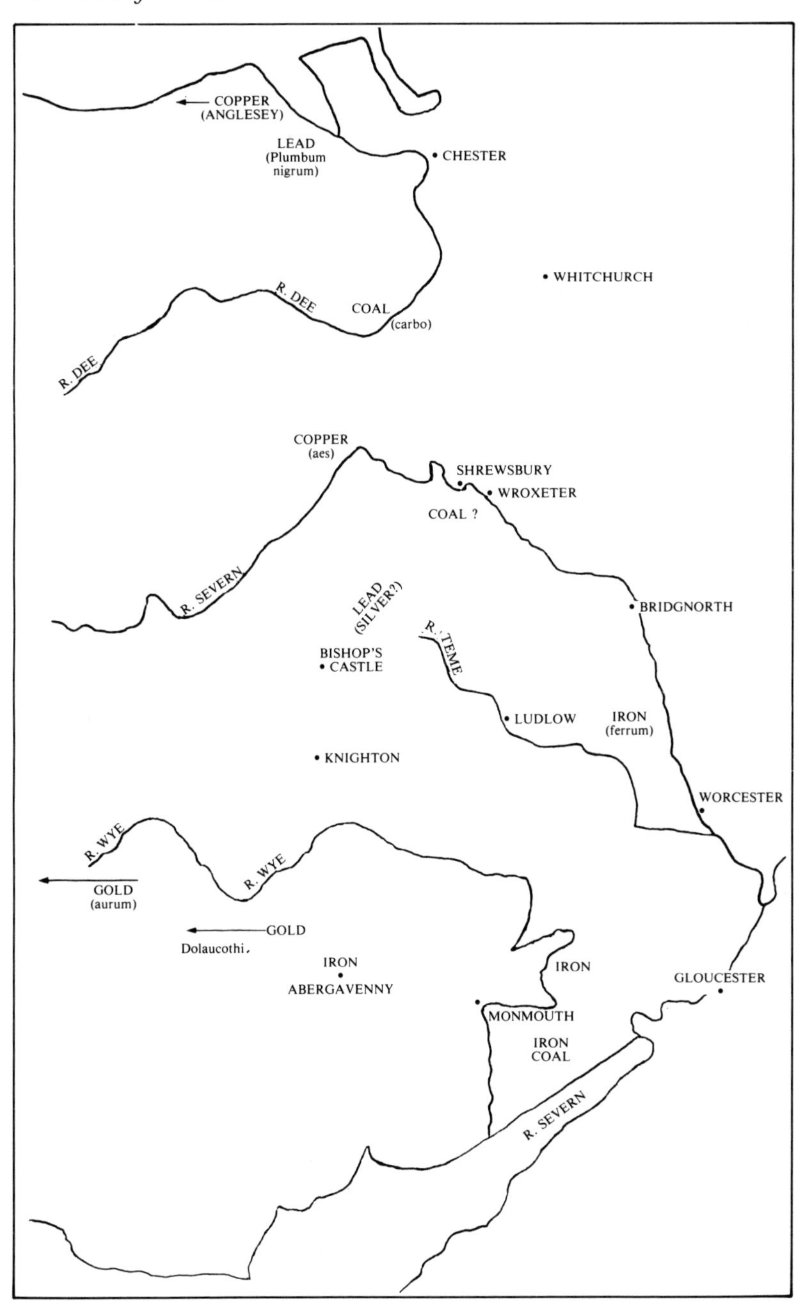

(ROMAN) BRITAIN: ORES AND MINERALS
IN THE BORDERLANDS

beibio), 'Rock of the crow or raven'. HANWOOD Sa (*Hanewde* DB) is 'Cock's wood' (OE *hana*), and this is echoed in ESGAIRGEILIOG Pow (near Llanwrin), 'Cock's ridge' (W. *ceiliog*). COED-Y-PAUN Gw (near Llangybi Fawr) means 'Wood of the peacock'. FULSHAW Chs (*Fuleschawe* 1252) probably contains OE *fugol* 'fowl', 'bird', plus *scaga,* 'wood', 'copse'.

Earthbound creatures play their part, too. We frequently encounter OE *dēor* which originally meant 'wild animal' but came to mean 'deer' - hence the word itself - in our modern sense. (Shifts of meaning like this - 'semantic' shifts - can be very important in the interpretation of place names.) Thus we have DEERFOLD He (near Lingen), DORFOLD Chs (*Derfold* 1360) - OE *dēor* plus *falod,* 'fold' - DEERHURST Gl, 'Deer wood', and DYRHAM Gl, 'Deer meadow'. The more specific OE *heorot,* 'hart', appears in HURSTLEY He (*Hurtesleg* 1242), 'Hart wood', in HARFORD Gl (*Heortford* 743), and in HARTFORD and HARTHILL Chs, the last three being self-explanatory. BUCKNALL St (*Buccenhal* 1227) and BUCKNELL Sa (*Buchehale* DB) probably contain OE *bucc,* 'buck', or *bucca,* 'he-goat', plus *halh,* 'retreat' - or Bucca adopted as a personal name.

OE *broc(c),* 'badger', was borrowed from Celtic *brokko-s* (W. *broch,* Gaelic *broc*), and some names in England containing this element may well have been in use before the Anglo-Saxon settlement (the BROCAVO of Roman Britain, in Cumbria, is taken to mean 'Badger-place'). However, another OE word *brōc* existed which became *broke, brook* in Middle English, giving us our modern *brook* in the sense 'stream'; and early entries showing *Broc-* do not, in themselves, help us to decide whether we are dealing with 'brock' (the badger) or 'brook'.

In fact BROCKTON Sa (*Brochetune* DB), near Lilleshall, BROCKTON Sa (*Brockton* 1272), near Worthen, BROCKTON Sa (*Brochton* 1252), near Lydbury North, BROCKTON Sa (*Broctone* DB), near Madeley, BRATTON Sa (*Brochetone* DB), near Wellington, and BROCTON St (*Broctone* DB) near Eccleshall are all close to water; BROCTON St (*Broctone* DB), near Stafford, is not quite so close. The first six, then, may well signify, 'Brook *tūn*' - but of course, even brocks may live near brooks, so the matter is not resolved.

One thing seems certain - that BADGER Sa, which we met in the Introduction, has nothing directly to do with brocks. But if - as has been suggested - the DB form *Beghesovre* and the 1255 form *Bagesover* mean 'Baecga's bank', it is possible that the name Baecga became confused with the word *badger* itself ('badged' or striped animal); such confusions are well evidenced in place names, and in this case there may have been a deliberate or unconscious association with the name of the BROCKTON a mile or so away.

The beaver (OE *beofor, befer*) is mentioned in BEVERSTONE Gl (*Beurestane* DB), as well as in BARBOURNE Wo (*Beferburne* 904), 'Beaver stream', while there is a (lost?) *Beuerton* in Herefordshire DB. PENMARK in Glamorgan may mean 'Head of the horse' - this type of name being not uncommon in Wales - while PWLL-Y-BLAIDD Pow (in old Radnorshire) is 'Wolf-pit' (W. *blaidd,* 'wolf'). HAREWOOD He (*Harewuda* 1138) and HARLEY Sa (*Harlege* DB) are probably both 'Hare wood' (OE *hara*), though the meaning 'grey' (OE *hār*) is not excluded as an alternative. The possible significance of HARGRAVE Chs and HARGREAVE Chs, both 'Hare grove', is discussed in Chapter 6.

As might be expected, trees are well represented - with the chief emphasis on oak and ash, though OE *beorc, birce,* 'birch' is found in BIRCHER Sa, BASFORD Chs (*Berchesford* DB), BIRTLES Chs (*Birchelis* 1260) - possibly 'Birch court', W. *llys* - and BERKELEY Gl (*Beorclea* 824). BOCKLETON Sa (*Boclinton* 1291) may contain OE *bōc,* 'beech', plus *hlinc,* 'slope' (the tree-name itself is descended from *bēce,* Middle English *beche* - a variant of *bōc,* which gives us our word *book* on account of the fact that beech-boards were once used for writing purposes).

OE *āc,* 'oak', is seen in the various Shropshire ACTONs (BURNELL, PIGOT, REYNOLD, SCOTT, ROUND, all but the last of these showing the addition of family names) as well as in ACTON BEAUCHAMP He and ACTON TRUSSELL St (which again record family possession). Here, OE *āc* has remained unchanged, or 'fossilised'*; but the Middle English form *ok(e)* is found in OCLE PYCHARD He, while OAKLEY names show the word spelt in the modern way, as does OAKMERE Chs. OAKEN St means 'at the oak(s)'.

It is certain that many OAK-type names were connected with boundary-marking, and the same is true of ASH names (OE *aesc,* 'ash-tree', Middle English *asch*). ASH MAGNA and PARVA Sa, near Whitchurch show clerical use of the Latin words for 'large' and 'small' respectively (see Chapter 1); ASH INGEN He records the family name Ingan. ASHFIELD Sa is self-explanatory, as are ASHFORD BOWDLER and ASHFORD CARBONEL Sa - two more family names having been appended

* Though the *a* sound has been shortened.

here. NASH Sa is a misunderstanding of *atten asche,* 'at the ash-tree' with the *n* becoming attached to the wrong word (Modern English *umpire,* from older *a nomper,* shows the reverse process). ASHBROOK Gl seems to be a misunderstanding of the *Astbrok,* 'east brook', entry of 1303.

W. *on(n),* 'ash-trees', occurs in the name of the river ONNY Sa and in that of ONIBURY, which stands on it. However, DB *Aneberie* for ONIBURY appears to show confusion with OE *ān,* 'one': and - in passing - this might explain ONE ASH Db (*Aneisc* DB) and the neighbouring MONYASH (*Moniasche* 1316), 'Many an ash', if the ONE in ONE ASH was originally W. *on.*

There were lime trees (OE *lind*) at LINDRIDGE Wo, maples (OE *hlyn*) at LINEAL Sa. Hawthorns (OE *hagaðorn*) grew at HATHERTON St (*Hagenðorndun* 996) - and indeed, both here and elsewhere they may well have been used for enclosures (see Chapter 8, THE BERTH). OE *alor,* 'alder' is contained in ORLETON He, Wo, OLLERTON Chs, and ARLE Gl. SAIGHTON Chs (*Salhtona* c. 1100) shows OE *salh,* 'sallow', while an OE form *willen,* 'of willows', may occur in WILLENHALL St; WILLEY Sa, He, Chs is 'Willow wood'. WYTHEFORD Sa and WITHINGTON Sa, He, Chs stem from *wiðig,* another OE word for the willow.

To set beside the plural W. *on* in ONNY and ONIBURY we find TREFONEN Sa, near Oswestry, 'Town of the ash-tree', *on(n)en.* LLWYNDERW Pow, near Welshpool, is 'Grove of the oak-trees', BWLCHYDDAR Pow (near Llanfyllin) is 'Oak pass', while DERWEN-LAS Pow (near Ysygarreg) is 'Green oak' (W. *derw, derwen, dâr*). TREWERN Pow (near Welshpool) is 'Alder town', while CASTELL COLLEN Pow - 'Hazel fort' - has already been mentioned. FEDW FAWR Gw (near Trellech) is 'Great Beech(es)', W. *bedwen* 'beech'. W. *coed,* 'a wood' is a common generalised element in Welsh place names - e.g. COED-DUON Gw, 'Blackwood' (near Bedwellte). CHEADLE Chs is bilingual, combining *coed* with an explanatory OE *lēah* (same meaning).

Before leaving the subject of trees (fruit trees have their place in Chapter 4) it should be mentioned that IRON ACTON Gl (*Irnacton* 1287), which contains both OE *īren,* 'iron', and *āc,* 'oak', is probably an example of topographical-type names with under-tones of activity. Domesday reveals that the men of Pucklechurch - situated about two miles from Iron Acton -rendered lumps or in-gots (Latin *massa*) of iron by way of dues; and the inference is that the oak-trees of Iron Acton were converted into charcoal for smelting iron in the locality generally.

We have already met with OE *brōm,* 'broom', in BROMLOW Sa; and the same element appears in BROOME, BROMFIELD and BROMDEN, Sa, BROMYARD Wo, WEST BROMWICH St, BRAMHALL and BROMBOROUGH Chs, and BROMSBERROW Gl. BROM-Y-CLOS He (*Broomy Close* 1650) is an amusing - and by no means uncommon - attempt to reconcile Welsh with English, since *brom* does not exist in Welsh as such.

Ferns (OE *fearn*) grew at FARLEY St (*Fernelege* DB), as they also did at FARLOW and FAIRLEY Sa, FARMCOTE Sa, Gl, and FARNDON Chs; the equivalent Welsh word, *rhedyn,* is found in TRERHEDYN, 'Fern town', in Dyfed. OE *fyrs,* 'furze', is seen in FRESELEY Wa, and in this case an early form of the Welsh equivalent *eithin* may ocur in IGHTFIELD Sa (*Ihtenefeld* 1260); in Powys, near Betws Cedewain, is LLANIEITHON, perhaps 'Enclosure of furze'. PREES Sa is W. *prys,* 'brushwood', and LUSTON He (*Lustone* DB) may contain W. *llus,* 'bilberry' (cp. BRYN LLUS, 'Bilberry hill', near Corwen in Gwynedd). Clover (OE *clǣfre*) flourished at CLAVERLEY Sa and at CLAVERTON Chs, while there were briars (OE *brǣr,*) at BRERETON Chs, St, and BRIERLEY St.

Here, then, are some of the natural growths which - in the form of place names at least - have become lasting features of the landscape; and of course, there are a great many more. However, whereas trees and plants may themselves disappear, in large measure this is not the case with the rocks and soils which support them.

Many of our modern terms for rock-types are either coinings based on Greek (like the word *geology* itself) or borrowings from other languages. (OE *clūd,* 'rock' has fallen out of use, the word *rock,* OE *rocc,* coming from Gallo-Roman *rocca; clūd* may appear in CLUTTON Chs, *Clutone* DB, but both it and *rocc* are uncommon in place names.) OE *stān,* 'stone' occurs frequently, but its exact significance is seldom clear. However, Old English does contain compounds like *cealc-stān,* 'chalk-stone', 'limestone', *gim-stān,* 'gem-stone' (Latin *calx, gemma*), *ceosel-stān,* 'gravel-stone', and a few others.

In general the Anglo-Saxons were no great builders in stone, if we exclude churches of simple type. And even here Ordericus Vitalis, the Shropshire-born monk who wrote an *Ecclesiastical History* (12th century) says that as late as the time of Edward the Confessor a parish church (St. Peter's) for Shrewsbury was built in wood - and that it was only in 1083 that his own father began building the replacement in stone which became the present

Abbey. Nevertheless, granted that the Saxons appear to have produced more carpenters than masons *(stān-wyrhtan),* stone was still required for millstones, whetstones, crosses, and other items.

As farmers, on the other hand, the Saxons will have needed to assess soil characteristics. OE *clǣg,* 'clay' (Middle English *cley, clei*) is not a borrowed word; nor is OE *clām,* which has the same meaning and which indirectly gave us the word *clammy,* 'sticky'. OE *lām,* 'loam' (clay and sand), another word of German stock, is related to OE *līm,* 'lime' - so here we find a reasonable degree of precision. As for *marl* - clay and lime - this word is probably of Celtic origin (cp. MARGIDUNUM), but came into English from late Latin *margila,* Old French *marle.*

Geologically-minded readers - not to mention farmers and agriculturists - will be better placed than the author to check rock-type and soil-type names against the facts on the ground in individual cases. However, to some extent and in different ways, names and 'geological profiles' do match up.

OE *cealc* is found in CHALFORD Gl (*Chalkforde* 1297), in a mostly limestone region. Clay-type names include CLEHONGER He (*Clehungre* 1236), CLAYHANGER Chs (*Clehongur* 1432) and CLAYHANGER St (*Cleyhungre* 13th century) - all meaning 'Clay slope' - and CLAYTON St (*Claitone* DB), which may have been associated with pottery. There is also sufficient clay, loam and marl in the general region of CLEE ST. MARGARET Sa (*Cleie, Clee* DB), CLEE STANTON Sa (*Cleie, Clee* DB, *Cleo Staunton* 1290), CLEETON Sa (*Cleoton* 1241, *Cletone* 1255), CLEOBURY MORTIMER Sa (*Claiberie, Cleberie* DB) and CLEOBURY NORTH Sa (*Ufere Cleobyrig* c. 1050, 'Upper Cleobury') to justify derivation of all these names from *clǣg* or *clei,* 'clay' (for the pronunciation *clee,* cp. CLEE Li, *Cleia* DB, *Cle,* c. 1115, 'Clay'). It seems possible that the entries containing *Cleo, Cleo-* have been influenced by W. *cleiog,* 'clayey'.

As for BROWN CLEE and TITTERSTONE CLEE (the hills), the 1232 entry is *Clivas,* OE *clifu,* 'cliffs' - but this name appears to have been ousted by one or other of the elements just listed for the local settlements. The area known as Dhustone, near Titterstone Clee, probably refers to the dark colour of the basaltic dolerite capping on the hill itself (W. *du,* 'dark', 'black'), for which the local name was 'jewstone'.

The element marl may appear in MARLSTON Chs (*Marleston* 1247). MARLBROOK Sa, on the other hand, is misleading in its modern form, since the 1195 entry *Marebroc* shows it to mean 'Boundary brook', OE *(ge)mǣre,* 'boundary'. OE *lām* is very difficult to distinguish from OE *lamb,* 'lamb'; but in the Borderlands neither element is relevant. As for the Welsh counties, their place names tell us little in direct fashion about soils - a fact accounted for in part, no doubt, by a tradition of pastoral farming.

OE *grēot,* 'grit', 'gravel' is found in GREETE Sa (*Grete* 1183), which is situated in an area associated by geologists with 'Head' - angular rock fragments resulting from the effects of glaciation. The same OE element accounts for GREET Gl, Wo, GRETTON Sa, Gl, GRATWICH St, and various other place names throughout England.

W. *graian, graean* and *gro* all have the same meaning as OE *grēot,* while *gröyn* means 'gravel-stone', 'pebble-stone'. Thus GRAIANRHYD, Clwyd, is 'Gravel ford'; NANT-Y-GRO Pow (near Llanwrthwl), GRONANT, Clwyd, and NANT-Y-GRAEAN, Gwynedd all signify 'Gravel valley', while GROFACH, Glamorgan, is 'Small gravel'. GRINSHILL Sa (*Grineleshul* 1242) possibly contains Irish *grinnell,* also 'gravel' (cp. CRUG GWYDDEL Pow, near Llandrindod Wells, 'Mound of the Irishman'). There is a quarry at Grinshill. FOEL GREON, Clwyd, looks like 'Gravel hill', 'Pebble hill'.

It has to be remembered that rocks of many different kinds, including gravels, are often brilliantly coloured - a fact of which pebble-collectors will be well aware; and before the end of the present chapter we shall be taking a general look at 'colour-type' names scattered throughout the Borderlands, since a fair proportion of these must owe their origins to the hues of local rocks (or soils).

However, the element *green* (meaning the colour) needs a separate comment. Readers may have noticed for themselves that various places said to be derived from OE or Middle English *grēne,* 'green' do not really seem to fit the bill; and it is distinctly possible that there have been confusions between the OE word (originally *grōēne*, cp. Old Norse *grōēnn*) and W. *gröyn,* 'gravel-stone', 'pebblestone'. This would apply particularly in areas where grass or other green vegetation is scarce, and so less likely to have determined a 'green-type' naming than other factors.

Thus at GRENDON GREEN He there is a 725 ft.-high outcrop of gravelly boulder-clay; here, then, the *Grenedene* of DB may signify 'Gravel valley', not 'Green valley'. CREW GREEN Sa, near Bausley, is in an area of hard, splintery volcanic tuff. GREEN HILL Sa, high up within the quartzite Stiperstones, is another unlikely candidate for a 'green' (colour) interpretation - unless outcrops of greenstone justify it. Near Bromyard, CRICK'S GREEN He is next door to the glacial gravels of

Newton Farm; while a few miles away, south of Suckley, we find GREENHILL next to STONY CROSS and GRITTLESEND - 'End of the grit', cp. GRITTLETON W (*Gretelintone* DB), OE *grēot-hlinc,* 'Gravel hill'. GREENHILL BANK Sa, near Ellesmere, is next to GRAVEL HOLE.

Certainly W. *gröyn* - or the OE *grēon*, 'gravel' suggested by Ekwall for ISLE of GRAIN K (*Grean* c.1100) - would go a long way towards solving the long list of GREEN, GREEN- and GREN- names for which 'green' interpretations seem inapt. Meanwhile MARIAN-GLAS, Anglesey, 'Green gravel', appears to provide us with the best of both worlds.*

OE *stān*, 'stone' is a common element, accounting for CLEE STANTON, STANTON LACY, STANTON LONG, LONG STANTON, and STANTON UPON HINE HEATH (all in Shropshire), STANTON Gl, St, STONE St, Gl, and many others of this rather unspecific type where stone buildings, stone ruins or even standing stones may have been involved. STANWARDINE Sa may mean 'Enclosure (OE *worðign*) made of stones'; while STANLOW Chs, 'Stony hill', STANNEY Chs 'Stony island' (OE *ēg*), and STANDISH Gl (*Stanedisch* 1291), 'Stony pasture' (OE *edisc*) again refer more plainly to the environment. STANWAY He was on a paved (Roman) road.

W. *maen*, 'stone' (plural *meini*) may be used in a topographical sense, as in PENMAENMAWR, Gwynedd, 'Great stone head' (site, incidentally, of a Neolithic axe-factory, from which specimen products have been recovered as far afield as Shropshire), or as referring to standing stones, e.g. LLWYNYMAEN Sa, near Oswestry, 'Grove of the stone', MEINI GWYN, Dyfed, 'White stones' etc. Or, as in OE, the reference may be direct to building material - hence combinations like PONT FAEN Sa, near Chirk, 'Stone bridge'. MAENDY and its variant TŶFAEN, 'Stone house', are both fairly common. GROESVAEN Pow, near Painscastle, is 'Stone cross'.

OE *sand,* 'sand' is found in SAMBROOK Sa (*Sambrok* 1285), 'Sand brook', SANDBACH Chs, 'Sand valley' (OE *baece*), SANDFORD Sa, 'Sand ford', SANSAW Sa (*Sandshawe* 1347), 'Sand wood' (OE *scaga*), and SANDON St, 'Sand hill'. The meanings here all seem to be primarily topographical; but there may be some overlapping with activity, since sand and gravel were used by the Anglo-Saxons to make mortar for plastering and flooring. The Irish *grinnell* suggested for GRINSHILL Sa also

* For what it is worth, there is an old Shropshire folk song entitled 'Green Gravel'.

means 'sand', and it may or may not be coincidence that Sansaw and Grinshill are close neighbours. W. *tywod*, 'sand' is not a common element in place names.

Turning to 'colour-type' names, we cannot expect the correlations with factors such as rocks, soils or vegetation to be consistent. Distance, perspective, changes of light and shade - all these must have affected the name-choices of settlers viewing localities for the first time. A. E. Housman's famous line asks 'What are those *blue* remembered hills ...?' - and we trust the poet's accurate eye precisely because far-off hills often *do* look blue, rather than green or brown or black. Even at more local level, green or red vegetation may grow on rocks or soils of the same colours - in places like Comley in Shropshire for example, where there is red limestone as well as red and bright-green sandstone. In short, we can seldom be absolutely sure why colour-names were bestowed.

That said, however, the fact remains that they are as plentiful in the Borderlands as everywhere else; and when dealing with them, it seems sensible to bear various possibilities in mind. For example, PITCHFORD Sa (*Piceforde* DB) is so named on account of its pitch (OE *pic*) or bitumen. But bitumen is black, so that nearby BLACKPITS probably owes its name to the same natural substance. On the other hand, both Pitchford and Blackpits are in the Coal Measures, providing another likely reason for *black* names in this area. Local or specialised knowledge, then, may have much to offer the dry bones of etymology.

OE *blaec*, 'black' became Middle English *blak, blake* (Chaucer uses the word *blake* to mean 'ink'), and so gives place names containing both BLACK- and BLAKE-; hence BLACKWELL Wo (*Blacwaelle* 964), 'Black stream' alongside BLAKENEY Gl (*Blachen* 1185, *Blakeneia* 1196), 'Black island'. The latter could be 'Blaca's island', showing a personal name; but it seems very likely that coal or iron is involved here, since Blakeney is on the very edge of the Forest of Dean (where some of the iron ore was still called 'blake ore' in the 19th century). W. *du* (plural *duon*), 'black' has already been met with, but it may sometimes take the form *ddu*.

Other BLACK- and BLAKE- names in the Borderlands are BLACKDEN, 'Black valley', BLACON (*Blachehol* DB), 'Black hollow', BLAKENHALL, 'Black nook' (these three are in Cheshire), BLAKEMERE He, 'Black mere', and BLACKFORD Sa (under Brown Clee Hill, an out-lier of the Coal Measures). Welsh names include the BLACK MOUNTAINS (MYNYDD DU), and large numbers of others referring to hills, rocks, lakes and so on - e.g. MOELYCERRIGDUON

Pow, 'Hill of the black rocks' (near Llanwyddyn), BRYN DU Pow, 'Black hill' (near Tregynon), DDUALLT Pow, 'Black slope' (near Trefeglwys), LLYN DU Pow, 'Black lake' (near Llanwnnog) etc.

OE *rēad*, Middle English *reed*, 'red' yields names showing RAD-, RAT-, RED- and REED-. It accounts for RADFORD Wo, RADMORE St, REDDITCH Wo and REDCASTLE Sa (*Radecliffe* 1227, 'Red cliff'). If Weston, near the latter, is indeed the site of Roman RUTUNIUM (Chapter 2), it is possible that an early form of W. *rhudd*, 'red' (Old Celtic *roudo-s*) may be involved in the ancient name; sandstone is prominent here - as it is at Stanton upon Hine Heath, another place proposed for Rutunium - and it should be noted that Latin *rutilus* (with *t*) also means 'red'. The *Radelau* of Hereford DB, which may be 'Red hill', appears to be lost; but some RAD-, RED- names are from OE *hrēod*, 'reed'.

REDBROOK Gw, on the Wye below the Forest of Dean, is an interesting name from the colour point of view. After snow or heavy rains, the Wye literally runs red here; and this must be due to the sandstone rocks and/or the red ochre in the limestones. The ochre itself was formerly used as a sheep-marking dye - hence, perhaps, REDDINGS INCLOSURE, a little further north in the Forest. To the east is RUDDLE - which, as it stands, also means 'red ochre' (from OE *rud*, 'red', or W. *rhudd*). The presence of red iron -haematite - in this ancient mining area is also to be borne in mind, and the same factor may apply elsewhere where RAD- or RED- names are concerned.

W. *coch*, 'red' occurs with some regularity in combinations such as CEFN COCH, 'Red ridge', RHOS-GOCH, 'Red moor', CLAWDD-COCH, 'Red ditch or dyke', ALLT GOCH, 'Red slope', MYNYDD COCH, 'Red mountain', BRYN COCH, 'Red hill', and so on. REDWITH Sa, near Llanymynech, may be bilingual 'Red lode' (OE *rēad* plus W. *gwyth* or Corn. *gwȳth*, see Chapter 4), referring to the copper-mining undertaken here from Roman times onwards.

OE *hwīt*, 'white', Middle English *whit* accounts for WHITCHURCH Sa, He, WHITBY Chs (showing Scandinavian *bȳr*, OE *by*, 'village' 'homestead'), WHITCLIFFE and WHITEFIELD Gl, WHITGREAVE St ('White grove or pit'), WHITLEIGH Chs, WHITMORE St and WHITTON Sa; but, as will have been gathered, there could have been more than one reason why these places were so named. W. *gwyn*, 'white' (this becomes *wen* after feminine nouns) may, again, be applied to various natural features, as in BRYNGWYN, CEFN GWYN, CARREG-WEN etc.

OE *geolu*, 'yellow' is not found, but W. *melyn* (feminine *melen*) is of frequent occurrence. FOWNHOPE He (*Faghehop* 1242) and FAINTREE Sa (*Fagentre* 1212) mean 'Multi-coloured valley' and 'Multi-coloured tree' respectively, from OE *fāg*. The equivalent W. *brith* (feminine *braith*) and *brych* (feminine *brech*) are also found, e.g. BRITHDIR, 'Multi-coloured land', FOEL-FRECH, 'Multi-coloured hill' - for (Y) MOEL-BRECH, showing the characteristic Welsh letter changes - and many others.

It remains only to say something about tracks and boundaries, which have a reasonable claim to be considered as enduring features of the landscape. OE *strǣt,* 'street' (an early borrowing), usually denotes a Roman road, and this is the meaning in all the STRETTON names of the Borderlands (except STRETTON Chs,* near Malpas) as well as in STRATTON Gl, STREET He, STREETHAY St ('Enclosure on a Roman road'), STREFFORD Sa, and STREETFORD He. W. *hynt*, 'road', 'track' is found in HINTS Sa, St; the Staffordshire Hints is on a Roman road, but it is possible that the Shropshire one was on a prehistoric track running from mid-Wales to the Severn near Bewdley. Another Welsh word for a road or track is *ffordd*; thus we find PEDAIR-FFORDD Pow 'Four-tracks' (near LLANRHAEADR-YM-MOCHNANT - 'Church of the waterfall in the pig or buck valley'), PENFFORDDWEN Pow, 'End or top of the white road', known in English as Staylittle (near Trefeglwys), and many other such names. W. *sarn,* 'causeway' is combined with OE *feld* in SARNESFIELD He.

OE *(ge)mǣre,* 'boundary' forms the first element in MAESBURY (*Meresberie* DB), MAESBROOK, MARRINGTON and MARLBROOK (mentioned earlier) - all in Salop - and MEERBROOK St. OE *mearc*, which has the same meaning, explains MARCLE He and MARPLE Chs (for *mǣrhop-hyll,* 'hill by the boundary valley'). The term MERCIA itself stems from OE *Merce,* 'boundary-dwellers'. W. *ffin,* also 'boundary', occurs in CAPEL-Y-FFIN Pow (near Glyn-fach), 'Chapel on the boundary' (i.e. the boundary between Herefordshire and the former Breconshire and Monmouthshire). The related W. *terfyn* occurs, too - as in NANT TERFYN, Clwyd, near Llansannan.

Finally, a word on the use of stones and stone crosses for the purpose of marking boundaries, crossroads etc. It seems extremely likely that OE *stān* in a name sometimes points to this

* This may contain OE *steorc*, 'young bull or heifer'.

kind of function, but in the absence of other evidence such instances are not easy to detect. The same applies equally to W. *maen, carreg,* and *craig* ('rock') unless they are used in conjunction with *ffin* or *terfyn* - which they seldom are. However, CRAIG ORLLWYN Pow (near Llansilin) does appear to be 'Rock (of the) boundary grove' (W. *or*, 'border', 'limit'). MAINSTONE Sa, He may be bilingual.

The symbolic use of crosses long pre-dates the Christian era (and the Greek Hecate was the goddess of crossroads) so that the mere presence of a word signifying 'cross' in a name does not itself rule out the possibility of a pre-Christian function such as boundary-marking etc. - even where churches now stand. The chief OE words meaning 'cross' are *cros* (Old Norse *kross*) and *crūc*, both words stemming from Latin *crux* (see Chapter 8). The relevant Welsh words are *croes* and *crwys*.

HOAR CROSS St (*Horcros* 1230) 'Grey cross' may record an ancient boundary, as may GROESLLWYD Pow, near Welshpool, also 'Grey cross', RHYDYCROESAU, Clwyd, near Llansilin, 'Ford of the crosses', and various other CROSS, CROES and CRWYS names; but their exact significance cannot always be determined.

CHAPTER 4

MAKING A LIVING

The value of Domesday Book in providing early forms of place names has already been stressed - and the value is, of course, all the greater where (as is often the case) the DB forms are the earliest on record. But DB entries as such are not solely concerned with place names; and it may be useful at this point to say a word or two about the sort of information they contain.

The survey of 1086 was primarily about taxation, i.e. about the extent to which settlements were 'geldable' (OE *geld,* Old Norse *gjelt,* 'payment', 'tribute'). Frequently the values of lands as at dates before or after 1066 (many areas had been laid waste following the Conquest itself) are given in entries beside the 1086 values; and we are told something about productive capacity and population, as well as about present and past tenants and subtenants. But although their style matches that of the *Anglo-Saxon Chronicle* for terseness, and although the details they supply regarding population are not easy to interpret, the entries as a whole can be of great interest in the context of place names.

Here is the entry for MILLICHOPE Sa, in translation from the clerical Latin in which - like all the rest of the survey - it was originally written:-

> 'The same Helgot holds [of Earl Roger] Melicope. Gamel held it [in Saxon times], and was free. Here i hide geldable. The land [is capable of employing] iii ox-teams. In lordship there is one [such team] and iii serfs. It was [formerly] worth 50s; now 15s.'

Now MILLICHOPE, which appears as *Millinghope* in 1199 and as *Myllynchop* in 1327, can be taken as standing either for OE *Mylening-hop,* 'Valley associated with a mill' or for OE *Mylen-hlinc-hop,* 'Valley by the mill hill'; but - assuming that the DB *Melicope* is a corruption or misunderstanding of whichever of the two later forms is to be preferred - there is no mention of a mill in the DB entry as such.

This may seem rather surprising, since mills strike one as being eminently valuable items and are, in fact, often mentioned in connexion with renders of fish (especially eels). But from the place name point of view, much of the fascination of Domesday lies in the ways in which entries do - or do not - harmonise with what the names themselves have to tell us.

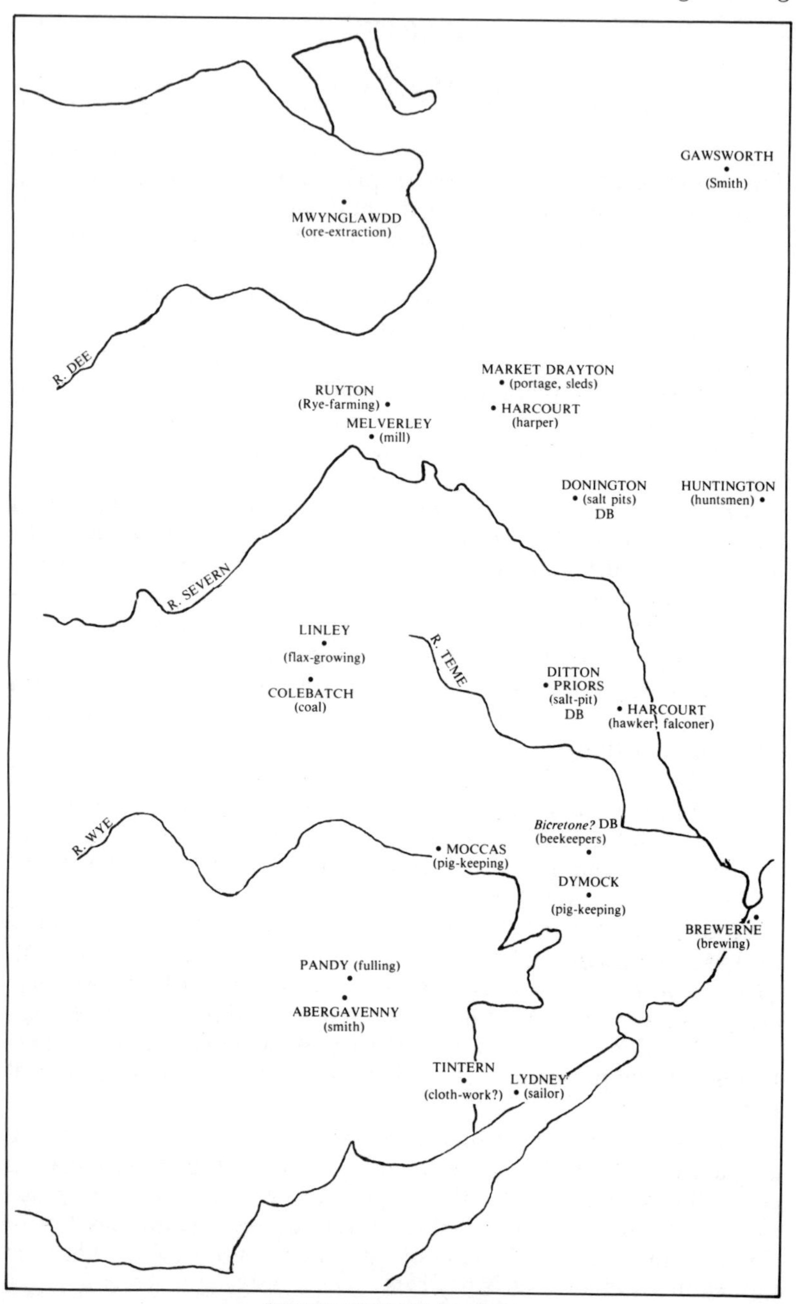

SOME PLACE NAMES SHOWING
OCCUPATIONS AND ACTIVITIES

Thus in some cases - as with MILLICHOPE - a name bears independent witness to an activity not mentioned in the entry concerning the place. In other cases we find the converse: the DB entry bears witness to an activity of which the name gives no hint, e.g. PUCKLECHURCH Gl (which, as we saw in Chapter 3, rendered 'masses' or ingots of iron) is OE *Pucelancyrcan* 950, 'Pūcela's* church' (corrupted to *Pulcrecerce* in DB). Occasionally, a place name and the entry concerning the place complement each other, e.g. RYTON Sa (*Ruitone* DB), 'Rye village', rendered eight sesters of rye (or wheat, Latin *siligo*) in 1086 and also possessed a mill - whose existence in this case might reasonably have been inferred. PRESTON GUBBALS Sa is among examples where name and entry directly corroborate each other; *Prestone* in DB, 'Priest village', this place was held in 1086 by the English priest Godebold, who lent his name to it (by 1292 we find it called *Preston Gobald*).

Here, then, are at least four different types of relationship between DB place names and the entries concerning the places - DB being taken as a convenient indicator. But it must be said that a name like RYTON is the exception rather than the rule; it is not often that we can say (as seems to be the case with Ryton), "Ah, yes - here is a place where rye was grown; it was named 'Rye village' for that reason, and it also had a mill to grind the grain." In short, although there is no lack of place names reflecting occupations and activities - ways of making a living - such names where they appear in Domesday are rarely backed up by the relevant entries.

On the other hand, DB statistics are themselves somewhat misleading. The surveys for the five counties of Shropshire, Herefordshire, Gloucestershire, Staffordshire and Worcestershire refer to a total of 1,711 rural settlements; but out of a total population of around 25,000, only 127 persons are classified as having what we might term skilled or semi-skilled occupations - as millers, salters, smiths, potters, reeves, bee-keepers etc. Yet although only four millers are mentioned (the only one for Shropshire was at STOKESAY - '(de) Sei's place' -where again the name provides no clue to his existence), more than 400 settlements are said to possess mills. In the same way, salt-pans are attributed to a minimum of 24 settlements, but mention is made of only four salters; while the case of fishers or fishermen is odder still, since for some 75 places with fisheries there is not a single reference to fishers - this in spite of FISHERWICK ST,

* 'Little goblin' - a diminutive of OE *pūca*, 'goblin', 'puck'.

which was firmly on the scene as *Fiscerwic*, 'Fisher-village', by 1167 at the very latest.

In view of this conflicting evidence as regards occupations and activities, there is a case for taking a fresh and much harder look at Old English and Old Norse personal names (including familiar names and nicknames), many of which have definite or highly probable meanings. For example, the personal name Lida suggested for LYDNEY Gl (*Lidaneg* 972) means (as *lida*) 'shipman' in OE, so that this place name can be quite correctly interpreted either as 'Lida's island' or as '(the) shipman's island'. However, there is a crucial difference between these two interpretations, as the reader can plainly see. For this reason, wherever an OE word customarily taken as a personal name in a place name has a known meaning which seems relevant, the meaning will be given in every case.

The importance of this is illustrated by another typical OE word, *smið*, 'smith', 'hammer-worker' (Latin *faber* in DB). This word has survived both in its own right and as a surname - Smith. But suppose that - as happened with OE *lida* - the word itself had fallen out of use long ago, and that its meaning had been forgotten. In that case, few people would be any the wiser for being told that a place name meant 'Smith's village' (with 'Smith' here put forward as a personal name).

Yet there is at least one place name in England - SMISBY Db (*Smiðesbi* 1166) - which could mean just that, the first element being either OE *smið* or Old Norse *smiðr*. It is really only because the word *smith* is still in use - and because evidence older than Domesday shows Anglo-Saxon England to have had plenty of smiths, including blacksmiths - that SMISBY is accepted as meaning '*the* smith's village' as opposed to 'Smith's or Smithr's village'. But again, if we think about it, what a difference there is between the two interpretations!

In the author's view, we cannot afford to ignore *any* known meanings of OE words in place names, even where the words may have been adopted or bestowed as personal names, familiar names or nicknames. If an Anglo-Saxon took or received the name Lida, 'Shipman', there is a good chance that his occupation was to do with ships (OE *lid*) - especially if he happened to live on an island. And the same goes for any number of other OE words put forward as personal names.

As it turns out, smith-ing itself provides an excellent starting-point for our survey of place names reflecting occupational activities. In 1086, at least 42 smiths were operating in the five counties cited above (no fewer than 25 of them lived in Herefordshire), and in a moment we shall be looking at the place names derived from the OE inflected form *smeoða*, 'of (the) smiths'. On grounds of antiquity alone, however, ABERGAVENNY Gw stakes a prior claim.

The place is recorded in the Antonine Itineraries (a collection of routes along the Roman Imperial roads in use during the first three centuries AD) as GOBANNIO; and this - whether it is a Latinised form* or purely Celtic - contains an Old Celtic *góbann-*, 'smith'. (The ever-helpful Caesar mentions a Gaulish personal name Gobannitio, which is obviously related and which may mean something like 'Little smith', or 'Smith-y' as a nickname.) Since Roman iron-workings existed at Abergavenny, it seems very probable that the name Gobannio refers to a blacksmith - a point which, in the light of the 'colour'- type names listed in Chapter 3, is well worth mentioning on its own account (cp. BLACKPITS Sa).

The place name GOBANNIO, having developed into GEBENNI, GEVENNI, was transferred to the river on which the present town stands - hence the late form ABERGAVENNY, 'Confluence of the Gavenny' (with the Usk). Meanwhile the original word *góbann-* developed independently into W. *gofan(n), gof,* 'smith'; but - as is always likely to happen - its former link with the name ABERGAVENNY was forgotten, a fact shown by the existence of a mistaken form Y FENNI ('The Benni' or 'The Fenni') for the River Gavenny itself.

The later Welsh word *gof* is found in GAWSWORTH Chs (*Govesurde* DB), 'Smith's, or the smith's, enclosure'; and this name is interesting in that the Old English possessive ending *-es* has been added to the Welsh first element, with OE *worð* completing the bilingual structure. It should be noted, too, that just as OE *smið* has given us the surname Smith, so has Welsh *gof* given us the surname Gough - indeed, as we have just seen, GAWSWORTH itself may have contained this name at least as early as 1086.

During excavations at CERRIG Y GOF, 'Stones of the smith', a barrow near Newport in Dyfed, traces of charcoal were found. It seems at least possible that the name preserves an ancient tradition, and that at some early period a smith or group of smiths used the charcoal for smelting purposes (cp. IRON ACTON Gl, referred to in Chapter 3). Meanwhile LLANYGOFAIN (LLANGOFEN) Gw, near Raglan, is 'Enclosure of the smiths'.

* The ablative case of a Latinised GOBANNIUM would be GOBANNIO.

English smith-ing names in the Borderlands include SMETHCOTE Sa (*Smethecot* 1242), SMETHCOTT Sa (*Smethecot* 1327), SMETHWICK St (*Smethewic* 1221) and SMETHWICK Chs (*Smethewyk* 1331). As noted earlier, each of these names derives from OE *smeoða*, 'of the smiths'; this explains why we find *e* in place of *i* - and also, of course, seems to indicate that in the places concerned we are dealing with groups or pairs of workers rather than with individuals (in Shropshire DB eight persons are categorised as smiths, but there is no mention of any at either Smethcott or Smethcote).

There is archaeological evidence for the use during the Saxon period of shaft furnaces in smelting operations, including the smelting of iron; and OE literature makes it plain that many smiths were, in fact, blacksmiths, producing a wide range of agricultural and other implements - including, of course, their own hammers, tongs and chisels. Wherever iron was smelted on a regular basis, large quantities of slag would have resulted; and in this context CINDERFORD Gl is of particular interest.

It seems that there were two places in the county bearing the same name. One, still on the map and situated in the Forest of Dean, was written *Sinderford* in 1258; while the other, now lost, lay within the boundaries of Pucklechurch and showed the form *Sinderford* as early as 950. Now we saw in Chapter 3 that Pucklechurch, which is not far from Iron Acton, was rendering dues of iron in 1086; and since the Forest of Dean has an iron-mining history stretching back to Roman times and probably beyond, there is every reason to think that CINDERFORD means 'Slag ford', from OE *sinder*, 'slag', 'scoria', 'clinker'. Slag was often used and re-used in smelting: indeed, as late as 1677 (according to a contemporary writer), *all* the iron produced in the Forest of Dean was made from cinders, i.e. the slag 'thrown by', as he puts it, in Roman times.

The name CINDERFORD has extra value in that it furnishes proof of the importance of semantics in place-name studies. For OE *sinder* later became confused with French *cendre*, 'ashes' (from Latin *cinerem*), thus undergoing a change of meaning as well as spelling. Especially in the light of the background facts, it would therefore be misleading to interpret CINDERFORD solely in terms of the word *cinder* as we now understand it. (Cp. CINDERS and CINDERS WOOD Wo, near Tenbury Wells.)

COLEFORD Gl (*Colford* 1534) is another interesting name. OE *col*, like Old Norse *kol*, signified both 'coal' and 'charcoal', so that COLEFORD could mean either 'Coal ford' or 'Charcoal ford'. In favour of the first meaning is the fact that the place itself is situated in the Coal Measures of the Forest of Dean - a reminder of how geological factors may provide clues. On the other hand, charcoal was always the preferred fuel for smelting; and if it was indeed charcoal that was made and/or carried at Coleford, some of it may have been destined for use at nearby Cinderford.

The 1534 form *Colford* is obviously late. However, COLEFORD So appears in DB as *Colforde*, which is identical in meaning and all but identical in form, so it is highly probable that the Gloucestershire name is much older than the 1534 record of it. Meanwhile, regarding the equally probable connexion with charcoal, it has been pointed out that the phrase 'wood and ironworks' which occurs more than once in the DB survey for Northamptonshire may well imply the production of charcoal for smelting purposes - particularly as the places for which smiths and ironworking are mentioned were all in well-wooded areas.

COLLINGTON He (*Collintune* DB) may contain the OE personal name Cola, giving the meaning 'Cola's village'. Again, however, Cola must merit consideration as an occupational name if it was derived directly from OE *col* so as to mean 'Coaly', 'Black'; and the same, of course, applies to the personal name Col taken as explaining COLEMERE Sa (*Colesmere* DB) - not far from Smithy Moor, where the local peat may have been burned for smelting - and COLESBORNE Gl (*Colesburna* c. 802), both these names showing the OE possessive ending *-es.* NANT-Y-GLO Gw means 'Coal brook' or 'Coal valley'. RHYD-Y-MWYN (Clwyd) is 'Ford of the ores or minerals' (type unspecified, possibly lead), and similarly we find MWYNGLAWDD, 'Ore or mineral pit', also in Clwyd (another name for this place is MINERA).

IRONBRIDGE Sa is a name of very late creation and requires no further comment. However, long before Abraham Darby came to the region, COALBROOKDALE (*Caldebrok* 1250) was already known for the coal which the great iron-master was to convert so profitably into coke. In 1322, one Walter de Caldebrook paid six shillings for the right to dig sea-coal at a place called LE BROCHOLES.

This place, which was probably near Madeley and therefore not far from Brockton (see Chapter 3), has exact parallels in BROCKHOLES La (*Brocholes* 1244) and BROCKHALL Np (*Brochole* 1220). These two names are both taken to mean 'Badger hole(s)', and perhaps they do mean no more than that. All the same - in the light of the said Walter's interest in digging for coal - it may be significant that the old lead-miners of the Stiperstones referred to their mines as 'setts' and 'foxholes'; and we may be a trifle naïve in thinking that settlements such as Brockhall and Brockholes - not to mention FOXHALL Sf (*Foxholes* 1325) and FOXHOLES La (same, 1325), among other similar ones - were named merely on account of commonplace animal habitats.

As for COALBROOKDALE itself, this is what is known as a 'popular etymology'. The 1250 form *Caldebrok* contains the Anglian *cald*, which gave modern English *cold* - hence the real meaning is 'Cold brook', with 'dale' added. Doubtless owing to the activities of Darby and his immediate predecessors, *cold* was later mistaken for *cole*, 'coal', 'charcoal' resulting in the present name. But the reverse process is also found: there are place names showing the modern form COLD for which earlier entries show *col* or *cole*, and names of this type are important in terms of activities. An excellent example is COLDRIDGE D (*Colrige* DB), 'Ridge where charcoal was made' (or 'where coal was found'). Borderlands examples may include COLDGREEN Sa, between the Titterstone and Brown Clee hills; and there appears to have been a widespread tendency to confuse *col* and *cold*.

The paragraphs devoted to iron, coal and charcoal will not be wasted if they help to convince the reader that there is no room for 'blind spots' where place names are concerned. The word *blacksmith* itself gives the clearest possible indication that an Anglo-Saxon did not need to have black hair or a dark complexion in order to adopt, or be given, a name like (for example) Blaecca, '(The) Black'; the reasons may have been rooted in practicalities, and these are worth investigating wherever possible. By the same token, a man named Hwita, '(The) White' need not have been fair-haired or pale. A *whitesmith* was formerly a worker in tin (which, incidentally, the Romans called *plumbum album,* 'white lead'); and it is not surprising to find two mines on the Stiperstones - WHITEGRIT and CEFN GWYNLLE, 'White-place ridge' - so called on account of what the miners termed 'white-rock veins', containing lead and barite. These Shropshire names may not be particularly old, but Romano-British VINDOCLADIA - representing old plural forms of W. *gwyn* and *clawdd* and signifying '(Town with) white ditches' - shows us that their type is not particularly new either. (Vindocladia was a fort built out of the Dorset chalk).

Returning to names of more straightforward kind, MILLINGTON Chs (*Mulneton* 1259), MILTON St (*Mulneton* 1229) and MILWICH St (*Mulewich* DB) all derive from OE *mylen*, Middle English *mille, mul(l)e* and mean 'Village with a mill', 'Mill village', and so can be added to MILLICHOPE Sa. MILFORD

Sa, 'Mill ford' was part of Little Ness, and DB tells us that this place did in fact possess a mill rendering 600 eels. WHELBATCH Sa (*Whelbache* c. 1275) signifies 'Valley with a wheel', and since DB refers to a seasonal mill here it seems likely that the OE *hwēol* in the name designates a millwheel. Nor should we forget Romano-British BRAVONIO or BRAVONIUM (now Leintwardine), which shows an early form of W. *breuan*, 'quern'; there was either a mill here too or the locality was a source of quern stones. FELINDRE Pow, between Knighton and Newtown, is 'Mill town' (W. *melin*, 'mill').

The grain taken to the mills of Anglo-Saxon England was mostly from rye, wheat and barley - especially the latter - and the cultivation of these cereals is duly reflected in place namings. RYTON Sa has already been mentioned, and rye was also grown at RUYTON Sa near Baschurch (Ruyton-XI-Towns), *Ruitone* in DB. OE *hwǣte,* 'wheat' (Middle English *whete*) is found in WHEATHILL Sa (*Whethull* 1237), while barley - used in the making of beer as well as bread - was the speciality at BARTON Chs, BARTON Gl near Bristol, BARTON Gl near Guiting, KING'S BARTON Gl and BARTON UNDER NEEDWOOD St, all these names showing OE *bere* or *baer* and meaning 'Barley farm'. OE *berewic,* 'barley grange' supplies the meaning of GREAT BERWICK Sa and BERWICK MAVISTON Sa. The last-named place may have had its share of disputes, since it owes the second part of its name to the Malveisin - 'Bad neighbour' in Norman-French - who held it in 1166.

The more generalised OE *corn,* 'corn', 'grain' could be the first element in CORNDEAN Gl (*Corndena* 1181), 'Corn valley', but here the 1207 *Querendon* suggests OE *cweorn,* 'quern', 'mill' - hence 'Mill hill' - which may also appear in the unidentified *Querentune* of Herefordshire DB. QUARNFORD St is 'Ford by a mill'. Grain was of course stored in barns (OE *berern,* Middle English *bern*), and this could explain BARNWOOD Gl (*Bernwude* 1221), cp. the Welsh YSGUBOR-Y-COED, 'Barn in the wood' of Dyfed (near Machynlleth). Cereal cultivation is not widely reflected in Welsh place names as a whole, though DÔL-HAIDD in Gwynedd (near Llangeler) is 'Barley meadow'.

The cultivation of fruit is attested by APPLETON Chs, which is OE *aeppeltūn,* 'apple farm', 'orchard', while APLEY Sa and APPERLEY Gl both mean 'Apple clearing'. Plums were introduced into Britain by the Romans, and OE *plūme,* 'plum' may appear in PLUMLEY Chs; however, this place is very near SMITHY GREEN, and it seems possible that the *Plumleia* of 1119 actually contains W. *plwm,* 'lead'.

Flax - used in the weaving of garments etc. - was grown from a very early period, and OE *fleax* is found in FLAXLEY Gl. OE *līn* also meant 'flax' - hence the word *line,* 'flax separated from the tow' - as did W. *llin,* and LINLEY Sa (*Linléé* c. 1166) near Bridgnorth, LINLEY Sa (*Linlega* c. 1150) near Lydbury, and LINTON He (*Lintune* DB) contain one or other of these words. Hemp was also grown from at least Saxon times onwards, and Middle English *hemp,* from OE *henep,* could explain HEMPTON Gl (same form, 1327), cp. HEMPSTEAD Nf (*Hempstede* c. 1130), 'Place where hemp was cultivated'. (The equivalent Welsh word, *cywarch,* occurs outside our area in GLYN CYWARCH, 'Hemp valley', near Harlech). Hemp was used to make cordage and fabrics.

Various names reflect animal husbandry, as distinct from the presence of animals which may have been wild - though in many cases the distinction is probably a fine one. Thus calves were reared at CALTON St and CALWICH St, both 'Calf farm', from OE *cealf;* sheep were kept at SHIPTON Sa and at SHIPTON (MOYNE) Gl (OE *scēap*), while DYMOCK Gl and MOCHDRE Pow (near Newtown) are Welsh 'Pighouse' and 'Pigtown' respectively; OE *gāt,* 'goat' is found in GATACRE Sa, 'Goat field', the Scandinavian equivalent *geit* in GAYTON Chs; the generalised OE *nēat,* 'cattle' explains NATTON Gl, and cattle are also implied in BINWESTON Sa, which shows OE *binn,* 'manger'; DOUGHTON Gl (*aet Ductune* 775-8) was known for its ducks (OE *dūce*) nearly 300 years before the Norman Conquest, and there were also ducks at DUKINFIELD Chs.

Middle English *bule, bole,* 'bull' implies the existence of an OE word *bula,* having the same meaning but not found except in place names. Thus BOOLEY Sa (*Boleley* c. 1100) and BULLEY Gl (*Bulelege* DB) are both 'Bull pasture'. STIRCHLEY Sa, containing OE *styrc,* signifies 'Pastures for bullocks or heifers'. BULLINGHOPE He may also contain OE *bula* (see BIRMINGHAM Wa, below, for place names containing OE *-ing*).

Cows were obviously an indispensable part of dairy farming (though goats' milk was also drunk), and it is reasonable to suppose that the cows at KEELE St (*Kyal* 1230), 'Cow's hill' and COOLE Chs (*Couhull* c. 1130), 'Cow hill' were used for this purpose. Certainly BUTTERTON St, showing OE *butere,* means 'Butter farm'; while at BUTTERLEY He and BITTERLEY Sa (*Buterle* 1242) the pastures were probably conducive to a good butter-supply. CHESWARDINE Sa (*Chesewurda* 1160) may contain OE *cēse* and signify 'Cheese farm'. Meanwhile HARDWICK, which occurs three times in Shropshire, and HARD-

WICKE, which occurs twice in Gloucestershire and once in Herefordshire, are from OE *heordwīc,* 'Farm for the herd or flock'. STOTTESDON Sa was *Stodesdone* in DB, showing OE *stōd,* 'stud' and giving the sense 'Hill for horse-breeding'.

Oxen would have been particularly valuable in Anglo-Saxon England as drawers of ploughs - indeed, most DB assessments speak of oxen or ox-teams, as well as of ox-men. OE *oxa* or the possessive plural *oxena* account between them for OXTON Chs, OXENBOLD Sa (*Oxenebold* 1205), 'House of the oxen', OXENHALL Gl (*Oxenhale* 1221), 'Retreat of the oxen', OXENTON Gl (*Oxendon* 1176), 'Hill of the oxen', and OXLEY St, 'Ox pasture'. UCKINGTON Sa (*Uchintune* DB) and UCKINGTON Gl (*Uchintone* 1221) may contain the Welsh plural *ychen,* 'oxen'.

Evidence for bee-keeping in the Borderlands is provided both independently by place names and also by comments in Domesday. Thus BICKERTON Chs and the *Bicretune* of Herefordshire DB are from OE *beocera-tūn* or *bycera-tūn,* 'Farm of the bee-keepers'. The Herefordshire region of Archenfield (whose name is derived from ARICONIUM*) merits special notice in that sizeable returns of honey as at 1086 were frequently made by Welshmen (DB *Walenses*); and it seems very likely that both here and elsewhere honey was fermented in order to make mead (OE *meodu,* W. *medd* - the latter word being found in LLANNERCH-Y-MEDD, 'Mead glade', in Anglesey). The Celts' fondness for mead was remarked on before the Christian era, but OE literature makes it abundantly clear that the Germanic peoples were no less partial to it. Honey was certainly produced at HONINGTON Wa - OE *Hunig-tūn,* 'Honey-farm' - and may have been collected wild at HONILEY Wa, 'Honey wood or glade', BEOLEY Wo, 'Bee wood', and BEOBRIDGE Sa, 'Bee bridge'. In early times honey was often used to supply the want of sugar, and hives were transported from place to place sometimes by water - cp. BICKERSTAFFE La, 'Bee-keepers' landing-place' - and this may explain HONEYBORNE Gl, 'Honey stream', and CHURCH HONEYBORNE Wo, nearby.

Both Celts and Saxons drank beer, too. The ear of barley displayed on coins of the British king Cunobelin (1st century AD) was partly intended as an advertisement for the island's own beer as opposed to imported wine; and it is very probable that BIRMINGHAM Wa (*Bermingeham* DB) can be explained in terms of OE *beorma,* 'barm', 'yeast' - an integral feature of both beer-brewing and bread-baking. However, an explanation along these lines re-

* An iron-working complex on the northern fringes of the Forest of Dean.

quires a few words about the OE particle *-ing* which appears in so many place names. The principles involved are not difficult to grasp, but rather a lot depends on them.

OE *-ing* had two chief functions. First, just as in modern English, it was used to form verbal nouns - *lǣring,* 'learning', *tǣcing,* 'teaching', *feorming,* 'farming', and so on. (Thus HUNTINGTON Chs, *Huntingdun* 958, may simply mean 'Hill for hunting'.) Secondly, it was added to nouns and adjectives so as to give the sense 'associated with' - thus *fēorthing,* 'associated with the *fēortha* or fourth part', i.e. 'farthing'; *faelging,* 'associated with the *fealg* or harrow', i. e. 'fallow-land'; *aeđeling,* 'associated with being *aeđel* or noble', i.e. 'nobleman'. The plural of this second type of *-ing* word was regularly *-ingas,* the possessive plural regularly *-inga;* so we get *aeđelingas,* 'noblemen', *aeđelinga,* 'of the noblemen' (which, incidentally, is found in ATHELNEY So, *Aeđelingaeigge* 878, 'Island of the noblemen').

What needs to be made clear is that two distinct methods of interpretation have come to be used in dealing with names of the *-ingas* and *-inga* type. The vast majority of such place names have been treated as though they contained personal names; accordingly BIRMINGHAM is said to mean 'Homestead of the people associated with Beorma' (a person not certain to have existed). But in complete contrast, HOVERINGHAM Nt (*Hoferingeham* 1167, understood as *Hoferinga-ham*) is said to mean 'Homestead of the people associated with the hump of land *(hofer)*'; while STONEGRAVE YN (*Staningagrave* 757-58) is said to mean 'Quarry *(graef)* of the people associated with stone *(stān)*'.

The reader will see that - as with Lida and *lida* in LYDNEY Gl - there is in fact a telling difference between these two types of interpretation. Grammatically speaking, however, the two types of name are identical, so that something of a problem presents itself. In the author's view, BIRMINGHAM ought first to be explained as 'Homestead of the people associated with barm or yeast' - since OE *beorma,* like OE *lida* in LYDNEY, has every right to be seen as a meaningful word.

As it happens, place names of the BIRMINGHAM, HOVERINGHAM and STONEGRAVE type are comparatively rare in the Borderlands. However, at the end of this chapter the reader will find more names on the LYDNEY pattern together with the meanings of their first elements, all possibly reflecting activities.

Meanwhile yeast or barm will certainly have been in demand at BREWERNE Gl - OE *brēow-aern,* 'brewery' - and presumably also at BAXTERLEY Wa (*Bakesterleye* 1282), 'Wood or clearing of the baker'.

Salt is one of the prime necessities of life, and its extraction and distribution rank among the oldest of all organised activities. The Romans operated sites for the evaporation and boiling of brine in many parts of Britain; and the importance of salt itself is of course shown by the fact that our word *salary* is derived through French from Latin *salarium* - originally salt rations, or money paid to the Roman soldiers so that they could buy salt.

DROITWICH Wo was one of at least three places called in Roman times SALINIS, '(At the) salt-pans', another of these being NANTWICH Chs. Both are situated in localities where strata of rock-salt give rise to numerous brine-springs, and both appear to have enjoyed a prosperity which continued up to and beyond the Norman Conquest.

DROITWICH was recorded in 716 as *Wiccium emptorium*, a curious form showing Latin *emptor*, 'purchaser' and perhaps meaning '(Salt) market'. In 888 it appears as *Saltwic* - which seems to indicate that OE *wīc* on its own does not mean 'saltworks', though it may have acquired that sense. In 1086 there were more than 200 salt-pans (DB *salinae*) at Droitwich, with many other salt-pans and brine-pits (DB *putei*) in the surrounding area. At Bromsgrove and Tardebigge the vats (*plumbi*) used to boil brine were made of lead, and it seems likely that the lead in question was brought to Northwick (probably the point of manufacture, since DB mentions a lead-works there) from the Stiperstones or from Cheshire. At Droitwich furnaces, burning either wood or charcoal prepared from it, were used to purify the brine.

The 1347 form *Drightwich* for Droitwich contains OE *dryht*, 'lordly', 'noble', while the *Nametwihc* of 1194 for Nantwich contains OE *named*, 'famous' - reflecting, perhaps, the importance of both places to the economic life of the Borderlands and the Midlands generally.

But while it is known that many Borderlands settlements had a direct stake in the great centres in Worcestershire and Cheshire, salt-extraction in the region was not confined to these two places alone. SALT St (*Selte* DB, *Salt* 1167) probably represents an OE *saelte*, 'salt-works'. WALLERSCOTE Chs (*Walrescota* 1186) shows a Mercian word *waellere*, 'salt-boiler', which survived in local dialect as *waller* and whose West Saxon equivalent, *wyllere*, appears in WILLERSEY Gl (*Wylleresege* 854), and these two names mean 'Salt-boiler's cottage' and 'Salt-boiler's marsh' respectively (Willersey is not far from Moreton-in-Marsh).

HARCOURT Sa (*Harpecote* DB) is derived either from OE *hearp*, 'harp' (i.e. the musical instrument, the Welsh word for which is found in TRE'R DELYN Pow, 'Harpton', in old Radnorshire) or from the OE *hearpe*, 'salt-harp' (an instrument for sifting salt) which has been taken as explaining SALTHROP W (*Salteharpe* DB). The element *cote* in *Harpecote* could mean 'storage-shed' or even 'workshop'; the latter sense would apply particularly well in names like SMETHCOTE, SMETHCOTT etc.* For obvious reasons, estuaries and other low-lying coastal areas were exploited in salt-evaporation - hence PWLLHELI, 'Salt-pit', in Gwynedd.

Wherever its point of origin, salt was transported far and wide, as is shown by names such as SALFORD Wa (*Saltforde* 1316) and SALTERS BRIDGE St - both self-explanatory. Names of this type (containing OE *sealt* or *sealtere*) have numerous parallels elsewhere in England, and there is every chance that WHITE, WHITE-, WHIT-, WHITT- names (containing OE *hwīta*, already referred to) would repay further investigation in terms of the salt trade - since salt was formerly known as 'white gold', owing to its value.

Two examples will suffice to illustrate the point. WHITEGATE Chs (same form, 1545) is in the right sort of area to have Scandinavian *gata*, Middle English *gate*, 'way', 'road' as its second element. (This sense of *gate* cannot be disputed, since in William Langland's *Piers Plowman*, c. 1377, we find *heighe gate* clearly meaning 'high road', i.e. 'highway'.†) Whitegate is within two or three miles of SALTERSWALL and roughly equidistant from Winsford and Northwich, both well known for their salt-production. Indeed, WINSFORD (*Wyneford bridge* c. 1334, *Wynsfurth brygge* 1475) may itself be Middle Welsh *Gwynffordd,* 'White way', or else show Gwyn adopted as a personal name (cp. GAWSWORTH Chs, above, for the addition of OE endings to Welsh words). Meanwhile WHITEWAY Gl lies on or very near a salt route running from Tewkesbury through Cheltenham and Leckhampton and on to Painswick.

But enough of salt. Another natural resource recorded in place names is woad, OE *wād*, and so we find WADBOROUGH Wo (*Wadbeorgas* 972), 'Woad hills'. The lost *Wadetune* of Herefordshire DB may be taken as containing the same element or a personal name, Wada, adapted from it. Woad was cultivated by the Saxons; and since there is evidence from the OE *Riddles*, written

* In German, *Hütte* signifies not only 'hut', 'shelter', 'cottage', but also 'foundry'.

† Passus 1V, line 42, B Text. Langland may have written some of his great poem at Cleobury Mortimer.

as early as the 8th century, that they used red dye in the making of bookbindings (they also called ink 'tree-dye'), it may reasonably be supposed that a place name like Wadborough directly implies the extraction of blue dye from the woad plant. A *Madrefeld* recorded c. 1211 for Herefordshire appears to contain OE *maeddre, maedere,* 'madder', which may also account for MADRESFIELD Wo (*Madresfeld* c. 1086). Madder, of course, yields a red dye.

Combs for the carding of wool are known from Roman times, and English *kember* is an obsolete word meaning 'wool-comber' (hence KEMBER WAY, near Penmark in Glamorgan). But the teasel, OE *tǣsel,* later *tassel,* was also used for the purpose of 'teasing' wool, and the OE word is found in TASLEY Sa (*Tasselegh* 1230). More recently, of course, carding was carried on in CARDINGMILL VALLEY Sa, and teasel-heads were still in use as late as the 19th century.

The stretching and combing of wool are part of the process of fulling; and it is possible that some teasels ('the fuller's herb', Latin *dipsacus fullonum*) found their way to the WALKMILL at Ludford bridge, on the Teme in Ludlow. The direct origin of this name is probably German *walken*, 'to beat', 'to press', hence German *Walker*, 'a fuller'; but we also find OE *wealcere*, 'fuller', which implies an OE verb *wealcan*, 'to full'. From one or other of these sources came the term *waulk,* meaning to work cloth up and down a board. There may have been fullers at WALGHERTON Chs (*Walcretune* DB, *Walcerton* 1260) - cp. WALKERN Hrt (*Walchra* DB), '(Of the) fullers'. Meanwhile Welsh PANDY Gw (near Crucornau Fawr) is 'Fulling-mill' - literally 'Beating-house', from W. *pannu*.

It has been suggested that TINTERN Gw represents W. *dinter(n)* for *deintur(n)*, borrowed from Middle English *teynter*, 'frame for stretching cloth'. Whether or not this is correct, the English word is the source of the figurative phrase 'to be on tenterhooks'.

The hides (OE *hȳd*, Middle English *hude, hide*) of cattle and horses, like the skins (Scandinavian *skinn*) of smaller animals, were used to make leather goods in Saxon England - hence, doubtless, the presence of skinners at SKINNINGROVE Li (*Scineregrive* c. 1175), 'Skinners' pit'. Untanned sheepskins and goatskins were turned into parchment, calfskins into vellum. But there is evidence for the existence of tanning-pits, too; and grave-finds have shown that, in addition to the bookbindings mentioned earlier, leather garments, bags, purses, wallets and shoes were produced. Thus archaeology confirms the statement (c. 1000) of the English monk Aelfric to the effect that the leather-workers of his day manufactured just this type of article, together with leggings, reins, halters, flasks and bottles. Other - and earlier -literary sources tell us that hides were also used in boat-building.

This background suggests that WEST FELTON Sa, FELTON BUTLER Sa and FELTON He (all *Feltone* in DB) contain OE *fel* 'hide', 'skin', rather than the OE *feld*, 'field' which is found in (for example) the 1082 form *Feldestede* for FELSTEAD Ess. FELTON BUTLER belonged c. 1165 to Hamo fitz Buteler - this personal name showing Anglo-French *buteler*, 'butler', 'bottler', which seems appropriate.* HIDCOTE Gl (*Hudicota* 716, *Hidecot* 1200) could be 'Hide workshop' (cp. HARCOURT Sa, near Wem, above).

Tanners, of course, need tannin, and virtually the sole source of this was oak-bark. As late as the 18th century the oaks of the Wyre forest served to supply the needs of the tanning industry at Bewdley in Worcestershire; while the tanners themselves lived on TANNER'S HILL and BARK HILL, on the outskirts of the town. (In Shropshire, near Wem, OAKLANDS WOOD and BARKERS GREEN are side by side, and here the second name may spring from W. *barcer*, 'tanner', though the word *bark* itself is an English borrowing from Scandinavian). The two Worcestershire names are late, but - as shown by FISHERWICK, WILLERSEY, RYTON, BUTTERLEY etc. - they are set firmly in an ancient tradition of linking place names to occupations and the products of labour.

The carriage of salt has already been referred to. However, Domesday makes it abundantly clear that a great many other labour-products were being shifted about quite freely both before and after 1086. Some, of course, went as dues to the king, but others would have been taken on a regular basis to markets and fairs; and it is likely that more than one market town grew up around spots long recognised as trading places.

OE *cēap*, 'barter', 'business' is found in CHEPSTOW Gw (*Chepestowe* 1308), 'Business-place' - effectively 'Market'. OE *cēping, cīeping,* '(place) associated with business' - a derivative of *cēap* and a good example of the second type of *-ing* word discussed above - occurs in CHIPPING SODBURY Gl, recorded as *Sodbury Mercata,* 'Trading Sodbury' in 1316. The word *market* itself, from Latin *mercātus*, has been added to certain names, including MARKET DRAYTON Sa, *Draitune* DB (see below). Another

* In 1242 the holder was Hamo *Pincernator* - this word also meaning 'butler'.

OE word, *byge*, 'trade', 'commerce' (hence our word *buy*) may be found in BYFORD He (*Buiford* DB), 'Trade ford', on the Wye.

OE *port*, from Latin *porta*, 'gate' also meant 'market', and this word may explain PORTWAY He (near Byford), NEWPORT Sa and perhaps NEWPORT Gw (*Novus Burgus* 1191) - though the latter, of course, is near the mouth of the Usk. W. *porth*, 'port' -i.e. 'harbour' - is from Latin *portus* (as is OE *port* in this sense); we find this word in PORTSKEWETT Gw (*Porth Isceuin* c. 1150), whose second element may represent W. *ysgawen*, 'elder tree'. (The place is on the Severn estuary). OE *faer*, 'passage', 'journey' (equivalent to Old Norse *far*) probably had connexions with trade - this is indicated by Old Norse *farmann*, 'travelling trader' - and forms the second element in HOLLINSFARE Chs, 'Passage by the hollies' (cp. the word *thoroughfare*). It is possible that Latin *nundinae*, 'market' is behind NAUNTON Gl, Wo, through the medium of early Welsh.

Some link between crosses and markets is indicated by CROSTON La, 'Village with a market cross' - a name echoed in the BUTTER CROSS of Ludlow (also Nottingham); OE *stapol*, 'post', 'pillar' may have the same sort of link, whose exact nature is hard to define but which could account for STAPLETON Sa, Gl. (Standing stones are to be borne in mind here, and the giving of names such as MERCHANTS' TABLE to megalithic burial chambers is probably not coincidental.)

The means of transporting goods included packhorses and packmules, carts, boats, and 'drays' (OE *draeg*), this term in some cases probably signifying 'portage' - i.e. a place where boats were carried or dragged past river obstructions or between two stretches of navigable water - and/or perhaps 'sled'.

Borderlands place names containing *draeg* include MARKET DRAYTON Sa, DRAYTON He, Wo, DRAYTON BASSETT St and DRAYCOTT IN THE CLAY St; indeed, this word almost uniformly gives names beginning with DRAY- or DREY-, and is responsible for at least 50 names throughout England. OE *mūl*, 'mule' explains MOULSTON Chs (*Multon* 1260), and it is not certain that the word does not occur elsewhere in the guise of a personal name, Mūl. Neither OE *craet*, 'cart' nor OE *waegn*, 'wagon' is evidenced in our area, but WANBOROUGH W (*Waenbeorgan* in an early charter) - 'Wagon hill' -may throw light on OE *draeg* as implying haulage up steep slopes. (There was a recorded *Drayhill*, 1399f., near DRAYTON Wa.)

The volume of traffic ought not to be underestimated. It is known from revenue returns that between the years 1179 and 1185 at least 200 cart loads of lead were carried away from the

Stiperstones, whose industry the Normans had revived. Some of this lead went to Shrewsbury, bound for Gloucester *via* the Severn; and Domesday tells us that, a century or so earlier, boats going up the Wye to the Forest of Dean - perhaps to exchange goods for iron or timber - had to pay toll at Chepstow. Waterways, then, were not unimportant; and particularly when dealing with place names involving roads, ways, tracks, fords, causeways, bridges, rivers etc. it is helpful to keep in mind the wide variety of people, produce, manufactured goods and general merchandise constantly moving along or over them. Within certain limits set by etymology, scope still exists for a dynamic (as opposed to static) approach to place names; for there are undoubtedly cases where a name in one locality appears to be connected with a name in another locality not far distant.

What emerges clearly from this chapter is that the uncomplicated reasoning behind large numbers of Old English settlement-names was no different from that which determined the naming of so many medieval streets and work areas. Every 'Mill village' (e.g. MILLINGTON Chs) has its parallels in namings such as MILL STREET, MILL LANE, MILL GATE, and so on. In the same way, 'Baker's clearing' (e.g. BAXTERLEY Wa) is paralleled by BAKER STREET, BAXTER GATE, BAXTER'S ROW; 'Smiths' place' (e.g. SMETHWICK Chs, St) by SMITH STREET, HAMMERSMITH, SMITHFIELD, IRON GATE, SILVER STREET; 'Stud hill' (e.g. STOTTESDON Sa) by STODMAN STREET; 'Rye village', 'Rye farm' (e.g. RYTON Sa) by RYE STREET; 'Market place' (e.g. CHEPSTOW Gw) by MARKET STREET, CROSS CHEAPING, CHEAP STREET; 'Charcoal place' (e.g. COLWICH St) by COWL STREET; 'Honey farm' (e.g. HONINGTON Wa) by HONEY LANE; 'Hound village', 'Kennels' (e.g. HUNTON Ha) by HUNGATE, HOUNDS GATE; 'Crock village', 'Pottery' (e.g. CROCKERTON W) by CROCK STREET - the list is impressive, and nearly everyone will know of other parallels.

Nevertheless, it is not nearly as impressive as it ought to be - the reason being the bias towards personal names, real or imaginary, which has already been mentioned more than once. Readers from PILKINGTON La (*Pilkenton* 1204) or PILTON Np (*Pilchetone* DB), for example, would be entitled to ask why their respective settlements are said to mean 'Pīleca's place' rather than 'Place where garments of fur or hide were made', showing OE *pilece, pylce*, 'fur garment', 'hide garment' - especially as PILCHER STREET (Nottingham) is so named precisely because garments of this type (Middle English *pilche*) were manufactured there. Grammatically speaking, no person called Pīleca is needed in order to make sense of either PILKINGTON or PILTON; while the evidence for Saxon tanning-pits, together with the existence of place names like SKINNINGROVE Li, can only serve to lend weight to a practical explanation.

We have already looked at a wide selection of names whose connexion with farming activities and products is generally accepted. But the balance is uneven. The Borderlands, like other regions, has its fair share of habitation names along the lines of PILKINGTON and PILTON in which the actual meanings of OE elements has been obscured. Since there is no clear-cut reason, linguistic or otherwise, why they should not be explained in the same way as - for example - COLWICH St (*Colewich* 1240), 'Place where charcoal was prepared', SAPPERTON Gl (*Sapere tun* 969), 'Place of the soap-makers', or WOOLWICH K (*Wulleuic* 964), 'Place where wool was handled', this chapter ends with a list of some of these names. (In this list, SHAVINGTON Chs means 'Place where planing-tools were made or used', BODENHAM He means 'Place where a messenger or beadle lived', and so on.)

BECKBURY Sa (*Beckebir* 1229), BECKFORD Gl (*Beccanford* 803) - OE *becca*, 'pick-axe', 'mattock'. BODENHAM He (*Bodeham* DB) - OE *boda*, 'messenger', 'beadle' (frequent mentions of beadles in Domesday include one for BODENHAM He itself). BUTTINGTON Gl (*Buttingtun* 894) - OE *bytt*, 'butt', 'cask'. CHILLINGTON St (*Chillentone* DB) - OE *cille, cylle*, 'leather bottle'. CHIPPENHAM Gl (*Cyppanham** 761-85) - OE *cȳpe, cȳpa*, 'merchant', 'trader' (cp. CHIPPENHAM Ca, *Cypeham*, c. 1080 and MANGERTON Do, OE *Mangera tūn*, 'Place of the traders'). ECCINGTON Wo (*Eccyncgtun* 972) - OE *ēaca*, 'usury' (cp. USURER'S MEADOW, field name, Shrewsbury St. Chad Parish).

HANHAM Gl (*Hanum* 1153) - OE *hān*, 'hone', 'whetstone' (cp. WHESTON Le, *Hwetstan* 1254, 'Whetstone'). INGESTRE St (*In Gestreon* DB) - OE *gestrēon*, 'profit', 'usury'. NAILSWORTH Gl (*Naillleswurd* 1196) - OE *naegl*, 'nail' (Domesday states that in 1066 Gloucester was providing rods of iron to make nails for the king's ships; Naegl here may be a good example of a significant nickname). PACKINGTON St (*Pakenton* 1166) - Old Norse *pakki*, Middle English *pakke*, 'pack', 'bundle'.

* CHIPPING La (*Chippin* 1203), from OE *cēping*, 'market', shows similar doubling of *p*.

SHAVINGTON Chs (*Shaventon* 1287) - OE *sceafa*, 'planing-tool', 'shaving-tool' (specimens of Saxon planes, axes, adzes, hammers and other carpenter's tools have been found). WORMINGTON Gl (*Wermetun* DB, *Wurminton* 1236) - OE *wurma, wyrma,* 'purple dye' (from the murex which yielded the dye iteself); from what we have already seen, 'Dyeing-place' makes perfectly good sense.

CHAPTER 5

MONEY

Stories about money and treasure are as old as the hills, and it is scarcely surprising that some of these stories came to embrace hills with barrows on them or that dragons (creatures of vast antiquity, see Chapter 6) were woven in for extra dramatic effect. Nevertheless - dragons notwithstanding - much treasure *has* been recovered from barrows, so that legend here has a solid factual basis. The chief problem where place names are concerned is knowing which names of the 'treasure' type resulted from finds already made and which from suspicions that treasure was still there waiting to be unearthed.

HORDLEY Sa is a case in point. In 1950 this place yielded a hoard (OE *hord*) of Roman coins, but it is not clear if the DB form *Hordelei,* 'Hoard wood', 'Hoard clearing' indicates that discoveries of similar kind had been made before 1086. (There may be a direct connexion between Hordley and the annal for 418 AD in the *Anglo-Saxon Chronicle,* which states:- 'In this year the Romans collected all the treasures which were in Britain and hid them in the earth...'; but again, there is no proof).

However, the Hordley coins at least serve to focus our attention on money itself - a very obvious form of treasure which, considering its importance, has been oddly neglected in the place-name context. The main aim of the present chapter is to look at ways in which money (from Latin *monēta*, 'mint') lays claim to be seen as part of our general place-name picture.

Before the start of the Roman occupation in 43 AD, the Celts in Britain had progressed from using ring-money (gold) and currency bars (iron) to striking coins of gold, silver, copper and tin at various mints which possibly included one at Cirencester. In addition to many others throughout the Empire, the Romans themselves had a mint in London and, in later years (it is thought), at both Cirencester (Roman CORINIUM) and Wroxeter. Following the withdrawal of the legions, however, coinage ceased for a long while to be the principal medium of exchange, though bronze coins were still produced to meet local needs. Except in former Roman centres such as Caerwent, barter may have been resorted to. On a small scale, then, we see here the history of coinage in reverse; for coins had their own origins in the practice of barter.

This ancient form of exchange, supplemented by the bronze 'coinage of necessity', continued for some 170 years. Around 580 AD, when the Anglo-Saxons had gained a firm foothold in the south-east, fresh Continental influence led to a revival of the coinage, with the mints of Canterbury and London leading the way. Gold was adopted as the standard, to be followed later by silver. In the third quarter of the 8th century AD, the silver penny (OE *pening*) emerged as the chief - indeed the only - coin in general use, and it remained so until long after the Norman Conquest.

We have been speaking broadly of coinage - but what, precisely, is a coin? To some readers this question may seem a rather odd one in the context of place names. Nevertheless, both directly and indirectly, the answers shed light on a surprising number of names, not a few of which are found in the Borderlands.

The number becomes less surprising when we remember one simple fact - that the making of coins is a specialised branch of metallurgy, involving smiths. In our own age of mass production, the average person probably gives little thought to how or where coins are manufactured. But originally, a 'moneyer' or 'minter' (OE *mynetere,* Icelandic *myntari*) was either a smith in his own right or a supervisor of other smiths; whichever of the two, he must have been a figure of some prominence - and not only at local level (in the early 13th century, one moneyer was Henry III's personal goldsmith). As such, he would have been a prime candidate where the granting of land was concerned - which opens up a genuinely fruitful line of approach to the question of personal names raised in Chapter 4. As we shall see, many personal names cited as explaining place names also turn out, on investigation, to be names borne by moneyers from the 7th century onwards. Considering the antiquity of the profession, and the likelihood of a hereditary system, this may not be altogether coincidental.

Returning to the coinage itself: our word *coin* is derived from Latin *cuneus,* 'wedge'. There are two possible reasons for this, perhaps not unrelated. One is that some early money-pieces appear to have been wedge-shaped, as we learn from the Bible.* The more likely reason, however, is that *cuneus* came to stand for the graving-tool used to cut designs on dies; by the time of the Norman kings the official engraver of dies was known as *cuneator,* and wedges are found as symbols on Saxon coins of the early 9th century.

* Joshua VII, 21: 'I saw among the spoil a garment and a wedge of gold ...'

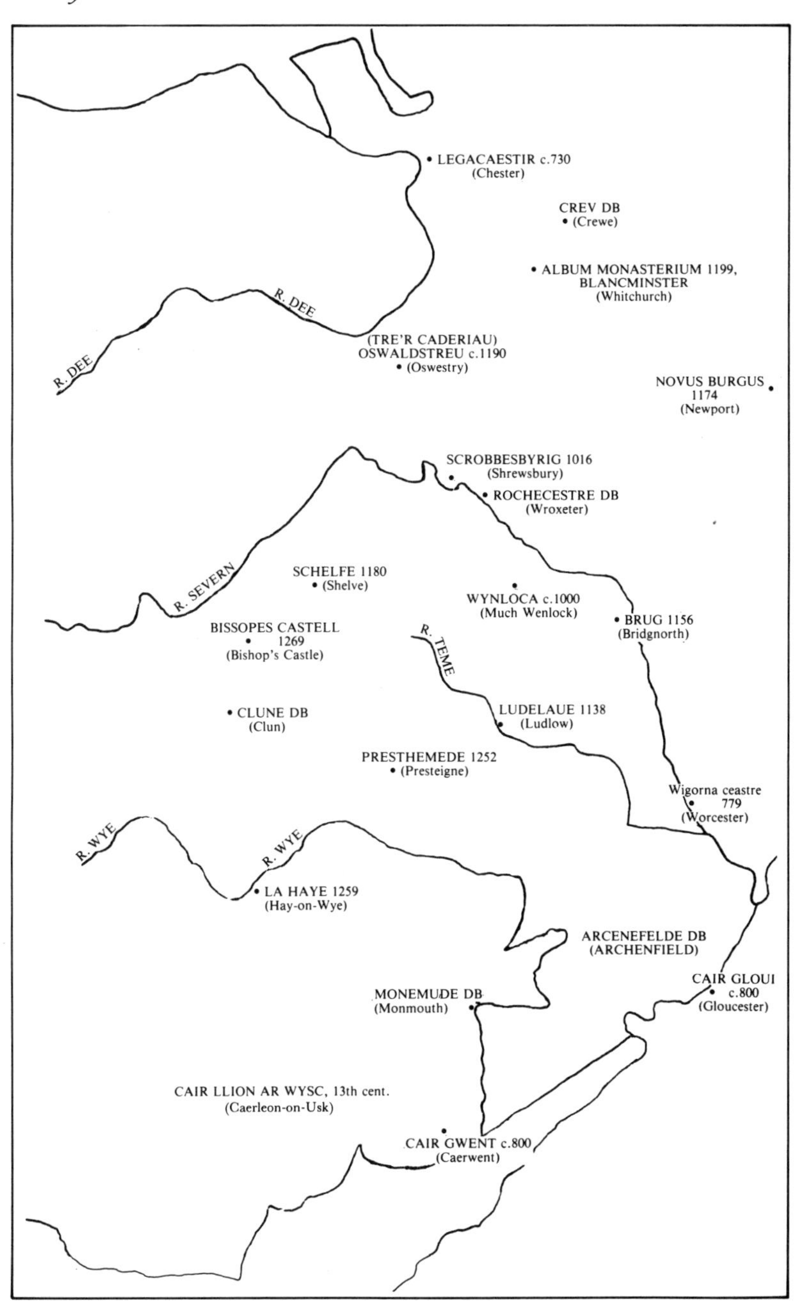

SOME POST-ROMAN FORMS OF
PLACE NAMES IN THE BORDERLANDS
(Clerical Latin, Anglo-Saxon, Anglo-French, Welsh)

By definition, then, a coin is something (it came to be metal) with a design struck onto it by means of a die; as with all metaphors, the expression 'to coin a phrase' is firmly based on fact. In Welsh, the words *bath* and *llun* respectively mean both 'shape' and 'coin'; and we find an early moneyer of Kent - perhaps of Anglo-Welsh stock - named Luning, which could mean 'Associated with coins'.

Some sort of traditional link between wedges of metal and actual coins may be traced in OE *wecg,* which signifies both 'lump of metal' and 'coin'. In the first sense it is roughly equivalent to the Latin *massa* met with earlier in connexion with PUCKLECHURCH Gl; and it would be interesting to know the precise reasons for the naming of CLIMPERWELL Gl, which contains OE *clympre,* also meaning 'lump of metal' (the same element occurs in CLIMPING Sx). Perhaps there was a well or spring here into which metal objects were thrown for luck; but the 'masses' of iron rendered at Pucklechurch make a connexion with metallurgy seem just as likely.

Equally there may have been a connexion with bullion and/or coins. It was long ago pointed out that, regardless of its size, almost any place with the *status* of a 'borough' - and this does not necessarily involve the occurrence of OE *burg/byrig* in the name of the place - may have had a mint at one time or another.* And where did the bullion needed for coin-making actually come from? Some must have been imported, and old coins may have been melted down and re-used; but by and large, this question is unanswered. Yet we have just seen that from about 775 AD onwards the chief coinage was the silver penny, and the quantities of silver required must have been large. Again, then, we cannot afford to pass up any clues - however tenuous - to be found in place names like CLIMPERWELL.

A further point to be made about the coinage is that neither the pound (OE *pund*) nor the shilling (OE *scilling, scylling, scelling*) was ever an actual coin until hundreds of years after the Norman Conquest. The Saxon pound of standard silver was a unit of weight *(libra ponderis)* or denomination of value, and there were 20 shillings - 'money of account' - to the pound; the number of silver pennies, or current coins, to the shilling varied between twelve, five and four. Probably long before 1066, at every recognised mint, the proper number of pennies to the pound of silver was tested at intervals both by means of scales (OE *sceala*) and by a melting-down process involving a furnace. (By the 12th century,

* F. M. Stenton, *Anglo-Saxon England,* p. 329.

this assaying process had been formalised into a ceremony carried out at the Exchequer in London). There was no coin called a shilling until 1548, while one of the earliest pound coins - of silver - was struck at Shrewsbury in 1642, during the Civil War.

None of this is irrelevant to place names, since *scilling* occurs at least four times as a place-name element and may well be connected with the production, storage or movement of silver bullion. Indeed, the OE word *scilling* itself may well be derived from OE *scill, scyll, scell,* 'shell', in the sense 'shell or scale of a balance' (this sense is actually evidenced in the early 17th century). When we reflect that OE *pund,* 'pound' is derived from Latin *pondus,* 'weight', and that Latin *libra* 'pound' also means 'pair of scales', we may feel that the meaning 'associated with the scales' is quite feasible for *scilling.* And, given the background facts, *Scillingas* as a Germanic group-name centred on bullion is not impossible; meanwhile the Norman personal names Schelin and Scilling are found from 1086 in connexion with SHILLING OKEFORD Do - near Shaftesbury, where there was a mint from 925 to at least 1154.

It was customary in Saxon times for moneyers to pay dues for the privilege of striking coins. As the separate kingdoms developed, dies had to be obtained from a controlled source; bullion for the mints, too, was supplied from centralised exchanges. But information as regards earlier days is scarce. Gloucester is known to have possessed a mint by 878 AD; by 925 or thereabouts mints were functioning at Shrewsbury, Hereford, Chester and Stafford, and after 979 at Worcester. However, large numbers of Saxon coins exist from periods earlier than any of these dates whose points of origin is uncertain. Not until the very end of the 9th century did all coins come to bear the names of both moneyer and mint; before that time, a coin might bear the names of king and moneyer only.

The kingdom of Mercia, whose supremacy began under Offa (757-796 AD), included most of our Borderlands region - and it was under Offa that the new silver pennies were introduced in about 775. Now the significance of this for place names is that the coins of Offa and some of his successors were struck chiefly by the moneyers of the Canterbury mint; and, later, moneyers of Canterbury, London and Mercia alike worked for the kings of Wessex.

Against this background, personal names known to have been borne by moneyers must be of potential interest when they occur in place names; and our next step is to look at a selection of such personal names scattered through the place names of the Borderlands. It is not, of course, suggested that moneyers were responsible in every case for the place names in question: that would be unreasonable. The sole intention here is to point out that large numbers of moneyers' names are on record, and to fit a wide range of place names into a clearly delineated and important context. (Who, for example, were the settlers at CONDERTON Wo, *Cantuaretun* 875, 'Place of the Kentishmen'? And it is worth noting that Plegmund, Archbishop of Canterbury from 890-914 - for whom the Canterbury mint struck coins - is said to have retired as a hermit to PLEMSTALL Chs, giving this place its name).

Starting with moneyers' names relevant to both Mercia and Kent within the 100 years following the first silver coinage of Offa in 775 (the dates of the earliest place-name forms are given wherever possible), Berhthelm is found in BRICKHAMPTON Gl and BRICKLEHAMPTON Gl (DB); Duda or Dudda in DERRINGTON St (DB), DIDLEY He (DB), EARLS DITTON and DITTON PRIORS Sa (DB), DINCHOPE Sa (c. 1180), DODINGTON Sa near Whitchurch (DB), DODINGTON Sa near Cleobury Mortimer (DB), DODINGTON Gl (DB), DUDBRIDGE Gl (1292), DUDDON Chs (1288) and DUDLEY Wo (DB); Ethelmōd in ELMSTREE Gl (962); Ethelstān in AUSTERTON Chs (1260); Lul in LULSLEY Wo; and Tīdbeorht in TIBBERTON Wo (978), Sa (DB) and Gl (DB).

Names of moneyers known to have struck coins for Mercian kings between 774 and 877 are found as follows:- Beornnōth in BARNTON Chs (DB); Cūthbert in COBERLEY Gl (DB); Dealla in Dawley Sa (DB); Dud and/or Dudd in DUDDESTON Wa (963) and DUDSTONE Sa (DB); Dudeman in DUDMASTON Sa (c. 1100); Dun or Dunn in DUNCHURCH Wa (DB) and DUNSMORE Wa (12th century); Eadwulf in ADLINGTON Chs (DB); Ealdwulf in AUSTREY Wo (958); Ealrēd in ALFRICK Wo; Eanbald in AMASTON Sa (DB); Eanrēd in EARDINGTON Sa (c. 1030); Tata in TADDINGTON Gl (840), TANNINGTON St (DB), TARRINGTON He (DB), TATENHILL St (942), TATTENHALL Chs (DB) and TATTON Chs (DB); Tatel in ADLESTROP Gl (1251) and TALTON Wo (991); Tīdhelm in TIDMINGTON Wa (977); Wine in WINNINGTON Chs (DB), WINSFORD St (1002), Chs (c. 1334) and WINSON Gl (DB); and Wulfeard in WOLVERLEY Wo (866).

After 925-935, when the coinage was regularised by Aethelstān of Wessex, minting was specifically limited to *ports* and to any place entitled to be regarded as a *burh*. It was henceforth customary - though there were numerous exceptions to the rule - for mints as well as moneyers to be identified on coins; the names of Shrewsbury, Hereford, Chester and Stafford now make their appearance, followed before the end of the century by Gloucester and Worcester. And again it is clear from a study of moneyers' names during this long period up to the Norman Conquest that some of them worked for more than one of these mints; while coins not showing mint-names do show the names of moneyers known to have worked at one or more of them.

Among the relevant personal names are Abba in ABDON Sa (DB) and ABINGHALL Gl (1165); Aelfwine in ALVINGTON Gl (1221); Boga in BOWDON Chs (DB); Bolla in BOLLINGTON Chs (1285), BOLSTONE He (1193) and BONINGALE Sa (1285); Cēnberht in KEMBERTON Sa (DB); Croc in CROXALL St (942), CROXDEN St (DB), CROXTON Chs (DB) and CROXTON St (DB); Dēorlaf in DARLASTON St near Stone (956), DARLASTON St near Wednesbury (1262), and DARLISTON Sa (1199); Eadmund in ADMASTON St (1176) and ARMSCOTT Wo (1042); Eadrēd in ARSCOTT Sa (1255); Eardulf in EARDISTON Wo (c. 957) and ARLESTON Sa (1188); Ecgheard in EGERLEY Sa (1245) and EGERTON Chs (1260); Gōda in GODLEY Chs (1285); Gōdrīc in GOODRICH He (1102); Hūnlāf in HULLASEY Gl (DB); Ifa in IVINGTON He (DB); Snell in SNELSON Chs (DB); Thurstān in THURSTASTON Chs (DB); Wulfsige in WOLSELEY St (DB) and WOOLSTONE Gl (DB); and Wulfstān in WOLSTANTON St (DB), WOOLSTANWOOD Chs (1316) and WOOLSTASTON Sa (DB).

The list could be much extended if the names of moneyers from other mints in England were included. There is no over-riding reason why this should not be done, since moneyers from, say, Exeter or Leicester or Oxford might easily have been granted holdings in the Borderlands; the advantage of the method followed so far is that the connexion between the Borderlands and moneyers bearing the names cited is solid. Nevertheless, study of the names of moneyers generally, by reigns, does create the strong impression that these were people who either moved about a great deal or had an interest in several mints at once. At all events they are thought to have lived rent-free and to have had certain rights of jurisdiction.

Before leaving the subject of real - as distinct from imagined or suspected - treasure, let us return for a moment to bullion. By the time of Aethelrēd II (979-1016) there were at least 75 mints in England, many new ones having been created in order to meet the Danegeld, or tribute-payments to the Danish invaders. It has been calculated that these payments amounted to 155,000 lbs of silver - more than 69 tons - involving, possibly, millions of coins. The conclusion must surely be that bullion, whatever its source, was being transported in all directions for conversion into coin; while even in normal times, of course, worn coins must have been melted down for purposes of re-issue. This gives new life to the OE term *mynet-smiððe,* 'mint-smithy'; and it is interesting to note from the laws of Aethelrēd himself that some moneyers worked 'in woods' *(inne wuda).* (Perhaps this explains the origin of the surname Wedgewood - see the remarks on OE *wecg* above).

Where silver is concerned, SILVERDALE St merits comment. Names of this type - cp. SILVERDALE La, SILVERLEY Ca, MONKSILVER D - are usually taken as indicating a silver or 'silvery' colour. But it may well be a mistake to take this sense for granted. In OE the words *seolfor,* 'silver' and *seolfren,* 'silvern' meant '(made) of silver'; the earliest recorded use of the word *silver* to indicate a colour seems to be in Chaucer (c. 1386). In Wales, rocks are often described as 'grey' *(llwyd),* but there is a notable shortage of rocks described as 'silvery' *(arianaidd);* on the other hand, W. *arian,* 'silver', is associated with real silver at CRAIG-YR-ARIAN, 'Stone of the silver', near Llandrillo in Gwynedd (where silver plate is said to have been hidden during the English Civil War) and at BONCYN ARIAN, 'Hillock of the silver' near Llanrhaeadr in Clwyd (where there is both a tradition of concealed treasure and also a robber's hole in the hillock).

The urban name SILVER STREET, referring to the activities of silversmiths, is fairly common throughout England. In London and Lincoln, however, the name dates from medieval times; and it would be interesting to know the original reasons behind the naming of SILVER STREET Gl, near DRAKESTONE, and SILVER STREET Wa, near DRAKES CROSS in Solihull. Middle English *drake* - denoting the male duck - may possibly explain DRAKESTONE and DRAKES CROSS; on the other hand, Draca, ('Dragon') was the name of a moneyer based at Winchcombe in Gloucestershire (1040-1042), and perhaps this ought not to be ignored.

OE *gold,* denoting the precious metal, is hard to detect with certainty in place names owing to the existence of OE *golde,* 'marigold'. Nevertheless, GOLDSTONE Sa (*Goldestan* 1185) could be 'Gold's stone' or 'Golda's stone'; there was a moneyer called Gold at Romney from 1087-1100, another called Golda at Axbridge from 1040-1042. (We may compare GOLDINGTON Bd, 'Golda's place', which is within the boundaries of Bedford - site of a mint from 956 onwards and not far from SILVER END.) GOLDCLIFFE Gw, near Newport, is said by Gerald of Wales to have taken on a 'golden sheen' when the sun shone upon it; however, he does add that it would be worth digging into its mineral deposits in order to investigate their nature - speaking, doubtless obliquely, of 'sweet honey'. (He refers elsewhere to silver mining at Llanelwy, or St. Asaph, near Rhuddlan in Clwyd, where there was a mint from 1087-1272 at least). Why GOLDEN VALLEY He (W. *ystrad aur*) is so called appears to be unknown.

It was seen at the beginning of the chapter that a hoard of coins was found at HORDLEY Sa, and that the naming may have been determined by earlier finds of a similar kind. We may conclude by mentioning one or two other places in the Borderlands which, although they have so far revealed nothing in the way of treasure, nevertheless bear highly suggestive names of the HORDLEY type. One such place is MONEY TUMP Gl, a round barrow near Bisley; but not far away is GOLDEN COFFIN FIELD, where another round barrow was at least believed to have contained the said priceless coffin. Comparison with MONEY HILL Hrt, near Therfield, where a round barrow yielded a number of copper ingots, and MONEYBURY HILL Bk, near Pitstone, where Roman and Celtic coins were found in yet another barrow, serves to indicate that the name MONEY TUMP may have had solid reasons behind it. GOLDEN COFFIN FIELD, too, may be compared with GOLDENLOW Hrt, near Gaddesden Row, where a valuable find was unearthed in 1290. (The proximity of all five sites to ancient trackways is worth noting).

It is now time to move on. We have already dealt with names reflecting ways of creating a livelihood, while in the present chapter we have considered money as the medium of exchange - restored, after a period of confusion, as an essential part of the social and economic fabric. But such matters are, of course, not the whole story. Beneath the externals of everyday life lurked the shadow of the 'old religion' - which, from the time of the earliest conversions, underwent a subtle process of absorption into the Christian framework. Much has been written on this fascinating subject, and in the chapter that follows we shall see how it, too, has relevance in the place-name context.

CHAPTER 6

'GREAT PAN IS DEAD'

At or not long after the time of the Crucifixion - according to a story in Plutarch* - a loud voice emanating from the Greek island of Paxi was heard to proclaim in dramatic fashion that 'Great Pan is dead'; and news of this happening eventually reached the ears of the emperor Tiberius (14-37 AD), in whose reign the Crucifixion is said to have taken place.

Striking though the story is, it nevertheless belies the facts. Great Pan - symbolising all those religions of the ancient world now described as 'pagan' - still had a long life ahead of him. It was only by the Edict of Milan (314 AD), following the conversion of Constantine, that Christianity was effectively endorsed as the official religion of the Empire; while the decrees abolishing paganism within the imperial boundaries were not passed until 380-390, under Theodosius I. During the preceding centuries more than one non-Christian emperor had authorised persecutions; in addition, there were fierce squabbles among the various regional churches - some involving heresies or alleged heresies, others the vital question as to which of these churches should exercise overall control.

Gregory the Great, Bishop of Rome from 590 to 604, more or less settled this last question in favour of his own see - thus deciding the future of millions. And it was by Gregory's order, of course, in 597, that Augustine was sent to convert the heathen English. Among them, as among other northern Germanic tribes, Pan still survived.

Meanwhile, however, the Celtic British Church already boasted a long history of its own in which the bishops of Rome had played no special part. One early writer (Tertullian) states that Christianity was active in Britain by the 2nd century - brought here, perhaps, by traders from the East, if not actually by converts within the legions. A Christian cryptogram discovered at Cirencester *(Corinium)* is thought to date from the 2nd or 3rd century; and tradition, at least, records the names of two Christians said to have been martyred at Caerleon-on-Usk *(Isca legionum)* in 304. These names, Aaron and Julius, are interesting by virtue of their being Jewish and Roman - as opposed to British - respectively; but the tradition is not clear as to whether the martyrs themselves were legionaries or citizens.

* *Obsolescence of Oracles,* probably late 1st century AD.

As for individual British churches at particular sites, there is no direct place-name evidence for their existence during the Romano-British period (43-410). But it is known that there were such churches; it has also been suggested that the element ECCLES or ECCLES- in certain names represents an OE version of an early Welsh *eglēs* (modern Welsh *eglwys*), 'church'. (The Welsh would have borrowed this word from Latin *ecclesia,* itself a borrowing from Greek). On the basis of this suggestion, ECCLESWALL He, ECCLESTON Chs, ECCLESHALL St, EXHALL Wa (*Eccleshale* 710), near Stratford, and EXHALL Wa (*Eccleshale* 1002), near Coventry are all taken as indicating the former presence of British churches at or near these places.

The actual naming of churches after martyr-saints became progressively more fashionable from the middle of the 4th century, when the first 'martyrologies' began to be compiled on a systematic basis. But this policy was initiated by the bishopric at Rome, and may not have spread to Britain as a whole until after the Synod of Whitby (664), at which the Celtic Church was forced to accept Rome's authority. In any case, those Celtic Christians who acquired the status of sainthood were not - necessarily - martyrs or workers of miracles; first and foremost they were founders of churches in their own right. Thus there are many places in Wales and the Welsh Borderlands which record the names of such founders or alleged founders (most of them now forgotten in practice) whose activities are in some cases said to date back to the 5th century.

Later in the chapter a fair number of these places will be listed. However, it seems a good idea to follow the logical order of things and deal first of all with the question of paganism itself. For of course, the vast majority of the Roman legionaries who began landing here in 43 AD were non-Christians; drawn from many corners of the Empire - auxiliaries from Thrace (Bulgaria), for example, served at Wroxeter, Cirencester and Gloucester - they imported their own brands of pagan belief to add to those already rooted in Britain. Almost up to the time of the army's departure in 410 or thereabouts, the old gods continued to flourish alongside the new Christian faith.

The cult of the emperor himself is worth a brief comment at this point. It has been suggested that AUST Gl (*Augusta* c. 1105) may be connected with Legio II Augusta, which was stationed for a while at Gloucester. But the fact appears to have been overlooked that the primary meaning of Latin *augusta* is 'sacred', 'holy', 'worthy of worship' - the reason why the title *augustus* was conferred on the emperor in the first place. Thus the name AUST may simply have meant 'Sacred', either in honour of the emperor (there were several names of this type on the Continent) or because the place itself, which is on the Severn or Sabrina, was already held sacred by the British. The name SABRINA itself, incidentally, became old Welsh HABREN, modern Welsh HAFREN - showing the normal change of primitive *s to h* in the Welsh tongue, with later change of *b* to *h;* the meaning of SABRINA is unknown, though it is possible that there was a water-goddess of this name.

As for the classical pantheon of Rome - Saturn, Jupiter, Juno, Minerva, Mercury, Mars and so on - they have left still fewer direct traces in place names of the Roman period than have Celtic gods of the same type. This is not really surprising, since it was not the Roman habit to name places in this way. But in any case, most of these well-known deities were evolved from still older forms of religion; behind them lies the welter of custom and superstition which the Roman poet Ovid describes in the *Fasti* (c. 8 AD) and which this poet's translator, Sir James Frazer, fitted into the vastly wider framework of his own work *The Golden Bough.* Taking into account this work and others influenced by it (not to mention the screen of camouflage erected by the Church), it seems unlikely that we shall ever know the full extent to which legend and superstition have influenced place naming as a whole.

In the present chapter, Welsh and English place names having pagan associations will be dealt with in a single block. This is largely a matter of convenience, and the reader is reminded that English - i.e. Anglo-Saxon - names of this type cannot have been bestowed before the middle of the 5th century at the very earliest (we cannot be so certain about the majority of Welsh ones). Some of these English names, no doubt, date from after the time of Augustine's mission (597) and carry derogatory overtones. By the same token, while some may refer to shrines erected by the Saxons themselves before their conversion, others are just as likely to refer to pre-existing sites of the Romano-British period. Nor should we rule out the possibility that, in certain areas, the Saxons may have been influenced by the pagan beliefs of their predecessors.

Names of unmistakeably Germanic origin include WEDNESBURY St and WEDNESFIELD St, both commemorating the god *Wōden* - the equivalent of the Roman Mercury, Welsh Merchur; here the original *ō* has changed to *e* just as in the day-name, Wednesday. FRETHERNE Gl (*Fridorn* DB) may contain the name of the goddess *Frīg* (counterpart of the Roman Venus, Welsh Gwener), who gave us our Friday, the meaning being

'Frīg's thorn-bush'. TYSOE Wa records the name of the war-god *Tiw* (Roman Mars, Welsh Mawrth), to whom we owe Tuesday. There is no apparent trace of *Thunor* or *Thor* (Roman Jupiter, Welsh Iau) in English place names in the Borderlands, and the same is true of *Saeter(n)** (Roman Saturnus, Welsh Sadwrn), *Sunne,* 'Sun' (Roman Sōl, Welsh Sul), and *Mōna,* 'Moon' (Roman Luna, Welsh Llun), though of course we still have Saturday, Sunday and Monday. Meanwhile GRIMSWORTH He, thought to be an old name for the hillfort at Credenhill, contains OE *Grīm* (Old Norse *Grimr*), a nickname of Wōden.

(The names of the days of the week are thus notable relics of paganism in themselves. Connected with the planets in an ill-understood way, they were not formally adopted into the Roman calendar until after the time of Theodosius, c. 400 AD, when they received the seal of Christian approval).

OE *wīh,* which originally meant 'holy', came to be used only in the sense 'heathen idol', 'heathen temple', and in this later sense it is found in WEOLEY Wo and WEEFORD St - 'Wood with an idol', 'Ford with an idol'. It has been suggested that an alternative form, *wēo,* may occur in WELLINGTON Sa, He.

Popular superstition is somewhat different from genuine religious belief - even if pagan - and the primitive fear of ghosts and demons probably belongs to the former category. Here would belong GRIMLEY Wo (*Grimanlea* 851) and GREENHILL Wo (*Grimanhyll* 957), which both contain OE *grīma,* 'ghost'. OE *scucca,* 'demon' is found in SHUCKNALL He, 'Hill of the demons', SHOCKLACH Chs, 'Demon stream', SHUGBOROUGH St, 'Demon fort' and SHUCKBURGH Wa, 'Demon hill'. (By Christian writers, *scucca* was sometimes used to mean 'The Devil' - i.e. Satan). PUCKLECHURCH Gl merits another mention here, since the personal name Pūcela recorded in it appears - as noted earlier - to be a 'hypocoristic' or 'familiar' form of OE Pūca, 'Goblin'. HAGLEY Sa (*Haggele* 1272) may contain Middle English *hagge,* 'hag', 'witch', as may HAGLOW Gl (*Haggelow* 1437). WICHENFORD Wo (*Wicheneford* 1204) may be either 'Ford of the magicians' (OE *wicca*) or 'Ford of the witches' (OE *wicce*), rather than 'Ford of the wych-elms' (OE *wice*). DRIFFIELD Gl (*Drifelle* DB) may mean 'Magician's field' (from OE *drī,* 'magician').

In considering Anglo-Saxon religious beliefs we must not forget their Germanic origins. The Roman historian Tacitus states in his *Germania* (98 AD) that the Germans were not much given to

* This name was borrowed direct from Latin before 449 AD. OE *Sunnan-daeg* and *Mōnan-daeg* are translations of Late Latin *dies sōlis* and *lunae dies* respectively.

building temples in the accepted sense; their 'holy places' were essentially woods and groves, and any idols they may have kept there were not given human likenesses. The Germans as a whole had great faith in omens and the casting of lots; for the latter purpose they invariably used branches cut from nut-bearing trees, while both the songs and the flight-paths of birds and - curiously - the neighing of horses were taken as providing favourable or unfavourable signs. (The horses concerned were specially kept in the sacred groves and woods). One method of forecasting the outcome of battles was by pitting one of their own champions against an enemy captive, in a kind of 'mock-run' of the real thing. Tacitus also says that the Germans practised human sacrifices, though only to Wōden (the Roman Mercury), and that their chief assemblies fell at the new or full moon.

As we shall see in a moment, it is unlikely that the pagan Anglo-Saxons had abandoned all these ancestral practices when they crossed the sea to Britain some 350 years after Tacitus wrote about them. For this reason, it is possible that HORSLEY He, 'Horse wood', has religious significance. OE *bearu,* 'grove' appears in BARROW Sa, Gl, as mentioned in Chapter 2; while OE *grāf(e)* or *grǣfe,* also 'grove', occurs in HARGRAVE Chs and HARGREAVE Chs, both 'Hare grove' (see below), GRAFTON Sa, He, Chs, and TEMPLE GRAFTON Wa - a significant name perhaps in that the Templars, who held this place in 1189, were (rightly or wrongly) often suspected by the Church of having pagan leanings. OE *hnutu,* 'nut' is found in NUTHURST Wa, (*Hnuthyrst* 704), 'Nut wood', and in at least eight other places in England. KEMPTON Sa is derived from the OE personal name Cempa, 'Champion'; THREAPWOOD Chs means 'Contest wood', from an OE word meaning 'to contest', 'to contend'.

Now while we cannot be confident that these names are - in fact - connected with pagan practices, it would probably be rash to say outright that they are not. At roughly the time (650) when the official conversion of the Anglo-Saxons was nearing its completion, Saint Eligius, Bishop of Noyon (formerly Noviomagus) in Gaul, preached a sermon to his own erring flock which has been recorded for us and in which some very unofficial beliefs come to light. Even at this late date he has to warn the people:-

1. Not to regard sneezing as ominous
2. Not to pay superstitious attention to the songs of birds
3. Not to plan journeys so as to coincide with the new moon
4. Not to celebrate 1st January (the last day of the old Roman Saturnalia) or 24th June ('St. John's Day') with profane ceremonies

5. Not to celebrate the coming of May (April 30 was the old German 'Night of Walburg' - later 'St. Walburga', whose name may live on in WALBERTON Sx, *Walburgetona* DB - the Earth Mother)
6. Not to worship moths or mice (cp. MUSGRAVE We, 'Mouse grove')
7. Not to pass cattle through holes in trees for superstitious reasons
8. Not to visit witches
9. Not to worship fountains or trees
10. Not to worship representations of feet (a symbol of the god Mercury) hung up at crossroads (themselves sacred to the Thracian/Greek Hecate).

These facts - many of which will be familiar to students of folklore - obviously represent only the tip of the iceberg, and we must not digress too far. However, it ought to be mentioned that the wolf, the goose and the woodpecker were sacred to Mars (who shares features with the Celtic Nodens), the oracular raven or 'black dove' to Apollo (the Celtic Mapona or Mabon), the cock to Mercury, the ram-headed serpent to the Celtic Cernunnos, the horse to the Celtic Epona, the dog to Nodens, the wren and the oak (with its rare mistletoe) to the Druids. The crane was associated with oracles and with the alphabet. Caesar tells us that the hare (see above, HARGRAVE, HARGREAVE), the goose and the chicken were already revered by the British before 54 BC; while various deities in the ancient world were portrayed with horns, a symbol of power. It can be seen, then, that at least some of the place names referred to in Chapter 3 may have more than straightforward topographical force.

WRENBURY Chs, 'Wren fort' is obviously English in form; but, like HARGRAVE and HARGREAVE, it may either be a translation of an earlier Welsh form or record a Welsh tradition. As just stated, the wren - known as the 'King of Birds' - was sacred to the Druids, and its ceremonial slaying on 26th December (St. Stephen's Day) was a custom which long survived in Britain generally.

Moving on to purely Welsh names, it is seldom easy to establish their true age, and for the most part the author has been content to give their meanings together with comments where appropriate. As with English names, some may be corruptions or adaptations of older forms; in general, however, Welsh names appear to have remained more stable over a long period of time than English ones.

MOEL DERWYDD, near Pentrefoelas in Clwyd, means 'Druid hill', and this is paralleled by BEDDAU'R DERWYDDON, 'Graves of the Druids', Dyfed, near LLANDEILO FAWR - which, perhaps significantly, is named after the 6th century Saint Teilo (or Eilau). The Druids are mentioned in some detail in Caesar's *Gallic War;* and bards (W. *bardd,* plural *beirdd*) were already associated with them by Roman writers in the 1st century AD. Thus in Powys we find PENTRE'R BEIRDD, 'Village of the bards', near Cegidfa, and in Gwynedd is MAEN-Y-BARDD, 'Stone of the bard', a megalith. (The linking of megalithic sites with the Druids is a tradition of long standing, but of dubious authenticity).

W. *gorsedd,* 'throne', 'seat' is likely to have bardic and/or Druidic overtones in place names, since the *Gorsedd y Beirdd,* or *Yr Orsedd,* is the great bardic institution. Relevant here are YR ORSEDD, 'The Throne' (English ROSSETT, showing the same sort of confusion between the two languages that we have seen before), BRYN-YR-ORSEDD, 'Hill of the throne', and PEN-YR-ORSEDD, 'Headland of the throne' - all in Clwyd. (The first and third of these places have tumuli).

LLYN Y TARW Pow, 'Lake of the bull', near Llanwnnog, NANT TARW Pow, 'Bull brook', south-west of Trecastle, and MYNYDD TARW, near Llanrhaeadr in Clwyd, 'Bull mountain' are worth noting. Bulls (W. *tarw*) are common symbols in many pagan religions; and the Druids, in particular, were said to drink the blood of milk-white bulls and eat the flesh as part of a divination-process involving dreams. Where names containing *tarw* are genuinely old survivals, it is worth remembering that, at approximately the time when the first Celts were colonising Britain, the sun at the vernal equinox was rising with the constellation Taurus, 'The Bull' - or at least was still traditionally supposed to be. Caesar says that the Druids were deeply versed in astronomy and gave lectures on the subject. (There are two stone circles at NANT TARW, immediately above which is FOEL DARW, 'Bull hill').

BRYN-Y-SAETHAU Pow, near Llangynyw, 'Hill of the arrows' is worth a mention not only because there is an ancient site here but also because arrows were commonly used in divination.* CWM IOU Pow, near Crucornau Fawr, may be compared with MAEN IAU near Enlli in Dyfed, the latter meaning 'Stone of Jupiter' (the Celtic Taranis) or 'Stone of the yoke' (W. *Iau, iau*). FOEL OFFRWM, near Llanfachreth in Gwynedd, means

* Cp. CNOCAN A CHRANUCHUIR (Arran), 'Hill of the casting of lots'.

'Hill of sacrifice'. ALLOR MOLOCH, 'Altar of Moloch', site of a megalithic tomb in Clwyd, presumably reflects knowledge gained from the Bible concerning the Canaanite god of this name (though there was also a 6th-century Irish saint named Moloc). NEBO, also in Clwyd near Capel Garmon, may be another Biblical name adopted for more pious reasons; if so, it is somewhat ironical that the original NEBO was itself probably named after the Babylonian Mercury. COELBREN Pow means literally 'Fortune-stick' - i.e. 'Lot', as in 'drawing lots'; this is another form of divination known as rhabdomancy.

FOEL WYLFA, near Llansilin in Clwyd, is either 'Hill of the watching-place' or 'Hill of the meeting-place' (W. *gwyl* or *gŵyl,* plus *-fa,* 'place'). It is reasonable to suppose that some 'watching-places' were used for observation of the stars or planets. TWYN DISGWYLFA Pow, near Sennybridge, could be either 'Hillock of the watch-tower' or 'Hillock of the observatory' - i.e. in the modern sense. BRYN-Y-GYDFA Pow, near Bugeildy (Beguildy) means 'Hill of the meeting-place', 'Hill of assembly' (W. *cydfa*). Names of this type could have Druidic or bardic overtones, since both *eisteddfod* and *gorsedd* (see above) can signify 'assembly', 'meeting', 'convention'. (TRE'R DELYN Pow 'Town of the harp' - English HARPTON - mentioned in Chapter 4, should not be forgotten here).

The Celtic goddess Epona, equated with the Welsh Rhiannon, daughter of the Lord of the Underworld, took the form of a horse (W. *march*); and this may help to explain NAID-Y-MARCH, 'Refuge of the horse' - name of a long barrow near Holywell in Clwyd. However, King Arthur's horse Cafall may be intended, as in CEFN CARN CAFALL Pow, 'Ridge of the cairn of Cafall', near Llanwrthwl. The wren (W. *dryw*) appears in CASTELL-Y-DRYW, 'Wren castle', 'Wren fort', near Llantriddyd in Glamorgan - the obvious parallel here being with WRENBURY Chs, already referred to. The blackbird (W. *mwyalch*) was also associated in Welsh legend with Rhiannon - she had three of them - and this may feature in TWYN MWYALCHOD Pow 'Hillock of the blackbirds', near Llanfrynach. Meanwhile CROES-Y-MWYALCH Gw, near Llanfihangel Lantarnam, is 'Cross or cross-roads of the blackbird'. If PENBLAITH (FARM) He is a corruption of PEN-BLAIDD, the meaning here is 'Head of the wolf' (this type of name may refer to animal sacrifice). The farm is near LLANGROVE, and this is itself a corruption of the English *Longe grove* of 1272, 'long grove'; as we have seen, such corruptions or confusions are not uncommon in the Borderlands. The Welsh words for grove - *celli, llwyn, coed, gwig* - are, like their

English counterparts, inherently note-worthy in place names, since woods and groves seem always to have had a sacred aura about them.

Thus Great Pan himself, with his horns, flute, goat's feet and alarmingly loud voice, was not only god of flocks and pastures - the shepherd *par excellence* - but also, like the Roman Faunus, lord of the woodlands, rocks and mountains. As a symbol of the fertility of nature, he seems to resemble the Celtic god Cernunnos, and may have survived into quite recent times as 'Jack in the Green'. But comparisons of this sort are not easy to sustain; even the deities of the Greeks and Romans share many features in common.

It is significant, though, that in Welsh the phrase *pibau Bugeilior* - literally 'pipes of the Shepherd' - signifies 'pipes of Pan'. (Another Welsh phrase with the same meaning is *pibau Nwython* - and we find a 6th century Saint Nwython who is said to have been the son of Gildas of the Golden Wood). Thus CARN-Y-BUGAIL in Glamorgan, 'Cairn of the Shepherd', near GELLI-GAER, 'Grove of the fort', may refer to no human shepherd, and the same may be true of BRYN BUGEILIAID Pow, 'Shepherd's hill', near Coelbren, and BRYNIAU BUGEILYDD, 'Shepherd's hills', in Gwynedd. BUGEILYN Pow, near Penegoes, appears to mean 'Little Shepherd'. (It is worth remembering that the traditional bishop's crook was essentially a shepherd's staff, or *crosier* - W. *bugeilffon* - and that the word *crosier* was later confused with Old French *croisier,* literally 'cross-bearer'). Meanwhile BUGEILDY (BEGUILDY) Pow and nearby CWM BUGAIL, respectively 'Shepherd's house' (W. *tŷ*) and 'Shepherd's valley', seem innocent enough.

As is well known, the Devil - like Pan - has goat's feet, and in some Greek accounts Pan is described as the son of a ram. Again, then, there are likely to be pagan overtones in namings such as CARN-YR-HYRDDOD, 'Cairn of the rams', near Llangeinwyr in Glamorgan, CASTELL-Y-GEIFR Pow, 'Castle or fort of the goats', near Ystradgynlais, and CARN-Y-GEIFR, 'Goats' cairn', near Llanwrthwl in Clwyd, and LLWYN-YR-HWRDD, 'Ram grove', near Clydau in Dyfed. Faunus, the Roman equivalent of Pan, was formerly known in Welsh as Coedior, 'The Woodsman', and GWYDDIOR Pow, near Llanbryn-mair, appears to mean the same (W. *gwŷdd,* 'trees', 'wood'). Another Welsh name for Faunus was Eleinon, meaning possibly 'Great Einon', and we find CAER EINON Pow, 'Fort of Einon', near Llanfaredd, and HEOL EINON Pow, 'Road of Einon', near Crickadarn.

Goblins or ghosts (W. *ellyll,* plural *ellyllon*) feature in BRYN-YR-ELLYLLON, site of a cairn near Mold, in Clwyd. ARFFEDOGAID-Y-WRACH, also in Clwyd near Llandynydd and also referring to a cairn, means 'Apronful of the witch' (W. *gwrach*). The lake named LLYN-YR-AFANC in the same county was reputedly inhabited by a monster - either a crocodile or a giant beaver, W. *afanc* - of vast antiquity. (Here, perhaps, is a Welsh equivalent of the 'sea-dragons', *sǣdracan,* observed swimming around the lake-hideout of Grendel's mother in *Beowulf*). This monster appears to have been known in other areas, for we find BEDD-YR-AFANC, 'Grave of the *afanc*', near Meline in Dyfed, site of a long barrow.

GWÂL-Y-FILIAST, 'Lair of the greyhound bitch' (W. *miliast*) occurs in Gwent as the name of a standing stone at Michaelston-y-fedw. Exactly the same name - a very curious one - is found in at least four other places in Wales in connexion with chamber tombs or burials chambers, and appears to be unexplained. A further three prehistoric sites contain the word *miliast* in combination with words signifying 'abode', 'kennel' and 'cot' respectively. It seems just possible that the greyhound bitch in question is the brightest star in the sky - Sirius, known to the Romans as Canicula, 'Little dog' or 'Little bitch'. As early as the 3rd century BC the Greek poet Aratus correctly described the 'Dog-star' as chasing the constellation Lepus - The Hare - through heaven for all eternity, and the astronomically-minded Druids may have shared this picture. (In English, incidentally, the word *greyhound* is misleading. It does not refer to colour, being derived from Old Norse *grey,* 'bitch', and *hundr,* 'hound').

Before moving on, it should be mentioned that wizards, magicians, sorcerers, soothsayers, diviners, charmers, enchanters, witches and witchcraft, cursing and blessing, necromancy (the raising of spirits), special kinds of magic involving poplar, hazel or almond branches, the profane use of oak and ash groves, the worship of idols on 'high places', omen-taking involving the use of sticks or arrows, and the interpretation of dreams and visions are all specifically referred to in the Hebrew Bible - some of these things being reflected in Biblical place names. Given the remarkable degree of similarity between pagan practices in the ancient world, it seems reasonable to suppose that many British place names now either lost to us or surviving in a Christian guise, together with others which now strike us as hopelessly obscure, will in fact have been connected with these practices.

As for place names commemorating saints, it is well known that Christian churches were frequently built at or near sites of earlier pagan worship. It is notable, too, in the saints' lives as presented to us, how often objects and animals known to have been revered in pre-Christian times appear with their rôles or characteristics subtly changed. No doubt many of the lesser-known saints were real men and women; but - even when we have discounted the more fabulous deeds attributed to them - it is still hard to know where legend stops and reality begins. For example, BRECONSHIRE (W. BRYCHEINIOG) is said to be named after King Brychan, 'The Freckled One', who had an Irish father and a Welsh mother. This may be true, but we cannot be sure that - as is also claimed - the 5th-century St. Cynog who gave his name to LLANGYNOG Pow (there are three such places in the county) was really the son of this marriage. (Cynog is said to have been killed by the Saxons at MERTHYR CYNOG Pow, 'Cynog the Martyr'). The 6th-century St. Illtud, too, is said to have been not only a magician but also a cousin of none other than King Arthur; in Powys - as mentioned earlier - we find his name in BEDD-ILLTUD, 'Grave of Illtud', a ring-cairn near Penpont which is close to a church dedicated to the saint, as well as in TŶ-ILLTUD, 'House of Illtud', a chamber tomb at Llanhamlach standing on its own.

W. *llan,* which originally meant 'clearing' in a neutral sense, came gradually to mean 'piece of special or consecrated land' (not necessarily Christian) and, finally, '(Christian) church'. At the majority of places whose names begin with LLAN-, a Christian foundation now stands. Usually this is a church, either founded by or dedicated to a saint; sometimes, however, the place is marked only by the tomb of a saint said to have died there, or by his cell or hermitage. Bearing in mind, then, that pagan, Christian and legendary elements are often likely to be mixed up together in their background history, places in the Borderlands containing LLAN- combined with the names of saints include:-

LLANAFAN Pow (St. Afan, 6th century); LLANANDRAS He, English PRESTEIGNE, 'Household of priests' (St. Andreas, i.e. Andrew, 1st century); LLANBADARN Pow (St. Padarn or Paternus, 5th or 6th century) - three different locations; LLANFRYNACH Gw (St. Brynach, 5th century, an Irishman); LLANGADFAN Pow (St. Cadfan, 6th century); LLANGATWG Gw (St. Cadog, 6th century - this name being a 'familiar' form of *Cadfael*) - three separate locations; LLANGURIG Pow (St. Curig, 6th century); LLANGYBI Pow (St. Cybi, 6th century); LLANGYNIDR Pow (St. Cynidr, 6th century, also known as St. Enoder) - site of a standing stone;

LLANGYNLLO Pow (St. Cynllo, 5th century); LLANDDEWI Pow, Gw (St. Dewi, i.e. St. David, 6th century) - at least ten separate locations (LLANDDEWI Gw is the English DEWSTOW, another example of confusion between Welsh and English; DEWSALL He, 'St. Dewi's well' and DEWCHURCH He show the same confusion).

At LLANELIAN in Clwyd (St. Elian, 6th century) there was a cursing-well, still in use at the end of the last century, into which pebbles inscribed with the victims' names were dropped; the well-keeper was paid a fee. LLANERFYL Pow is named after St. Erfyl, date unknown. There are also LLANIDLOES Pow (St. Idloes, 7th century); LLANLLWCHAIARN Pow (St. Llwchaiarn, 6th century); LLANFIHANGEL Pow, Gw, Clwyd (St. Michael the Archangel) - a great many different locations, sometimes LLANVIHANGEL; LLANFYLLIN Pow (St. Myllin, date uncertain); LLANBEDR Pow, Gw, Clwyd (St. Peter, 1st century) - different locations; LLANDRILLO, Clwyd (St. Trillo, 6th century); LLANWRTHWL Pow (St. Wrthwl, date uncertain); LLANWYDDELAN Pow (St. Gwyddelan, date uncertain).

LLANFAIR- in a Welsh place name means 'Church of St. Mary' (W. Mair), and of course occurs many times. LLAN-SANFFRAID is also frequent and means 'Church of St. Bridget, St. Bride' (W. Ffraid), said to represent an earlier Brigid or Brigit, fertility goddess and patroness of poets, healers and smiths; BRIDSTOW He also contains the name of this saint. LLANDRINDOD Pow is 'Church of the Trinity' (W. *Trindod*), and is paralleled by EGLWYS-Y-DRINDOD Gw, 'Church of the Trinity'. LLANTRISAINT Gw is 'Church of the three saints'. (PUMSAINT, 'Five saints', in Dyfed commemorates the five saintly sons of Cynyr - a British chieftain of the 5th century - who are said to sleep beneath a rock in the former Roman gold mines at nearby Dolaucothi, mentioned in Chapter 1).

Place names beginning with the word SAINT (from Latin *sanctus*) followed by the relevant Celtic personal name include ST. BRIAVELS Gl, in the Forest of Dean area. This appears to refer to the 6th-century Breton saint, Brioch or Briog, whose name in this form is an abbreviation of Briafael (possibly from earlier Britomaglos). ST. CLODOCK He commemorates St. Clydog. SELLACK He is a corruption of the name Suluc - itself a 'familiar' form of the name of St. Silio, found in LLANDYSILIO Pow; this represents W. *ty-Silio, ty* having the sense 'your' as in 'your lordship' etc., hence 'Church of your Silio'. KENDER-CHURCH He contains the name of St. Cynidr.

Saints' names are found in combination with Welsh elements other than *llan*. Some fountains, springs or wells (W. *ffynnon*) which were probably held sacred in pre-Christian times now have a Christian flavour. Thus FFYNNON GARMON in Clwyd is 'Well or fountain of St. Garmon' (St. Germanus of Auxerre, 5th century), while FFYNNON ILLOG Pow and FYNNON DOGFAN Pow are associated with St. Illog (7th century) and St. Dogfan (5th century) respectively. At Meifod, also in Powys, is GWELY GWYDDFARCH, 'Resting-place of St. Gwyddfarch' (whose name means 'Warship' - literally, 'Wooden horse'), site of an oratory or small chapel. The Welsh word for chapel, *capel,* is found in CAPEL GARMON, in Clwyd; but, like *eglwys,* 'church', it is less common in combination with saints' names than *llan*. As we have seen, cairns, tumuli etc. are sometimes depicted as the graves or houses of saints, but purely natural features are seldom treated in this Christianising way. When *llan* is used in combination with saintly names - as is the general rule - some extra detail is sometimes added, e.g. LLANDDEWI'R-CWM Pow, 'Church of St. Dewi (St. David) in the valley'. Only rarely is *llan* found directly combined with topographical words, as in LLANRHAEADR Pow, 'Church of or by the waterfall', already mentioned.

It can be seen that - with the notable exceptions of St. Mary, St. Peter and St. Michael - Welsh churches and the localities in which they stand tend to be named after founders and patrons of native (or at least Celtic) origin. This is much less often the case with churches in England. The Anglo-Saxons owed their conversion almost exclusively to Rome through the agency of St. Augustine and those who followed him. As a result, large numbers of English churches came to be dedicated to saints figuring prominently in the Roman martyrologies - many of these saints, St. George included, having their origins in the Near East. Nevertheless, English evangelists and martyrs were not altogether lacking; and they, too, have left their names on the map of the Borderlands.

Of obvious importance here is St. Chad (OE *Ceadda*), who founded the bishopric of Lichfield in 669 and who was instrumental in the conversion of the Mercian people. CHADWICK Wo (*Cheddewic* 1182) may contain either Chad's name or that of his brother, St. Cedd. CHADSHUNT Wa (*Chaddeleshunt* c. 1050, *Chedelesfont* 1135), 'Ceaddel's spring or well', is interesting in that it may genuinely contain Chad's own name in its 'familiar' form, Ceaddel. If so, this would explain the former presence here of a well and an oratory, both dedicated to the saint, which brought the local priest an income of £16 a year from the offerings of pilgrims. If not, there may have been ecclesiastical exploitation of the fact that the settlement-name echoed that of Chad (the reader may recall the 'pious fraud' involving the bones unearthed at Ludlow, mentioned in Chapter 2). CHADWICH Wo (*Chadeleswick* 1212) and CHADWICK Wa (*Chadeleswiz* 1242) could, again, be connected with Chad, while CHADKIRK Chs is 'Chad's church'.

LICHFIELD St, British LETOCETO, 'Grey wood', 'Grey grove' merits a further mention here. If this wood or grove was originally an important site of pagan worship, recognised as such by the pagan Mercians, then Chad would have had sound reasons for establishing his bishopric at this precise place - just as the Romans before him, perhaps, had equally sound reasons for building their fort at nearby Wall (see Chapter 2).

CHADBURY Wo (*Ceadwallan byrig* c. 860) is definitely not connected with St. Chad, as the early form shows. Ceadwalla was the name of a particularly bloodthirsty West Saxon king of the 7th century; but he was baptised towards the end of his life and then made a saint. It seems rather unlikely that this place name refers to the king in his saintly capacity.

By contrast, STOKE ST. MILBOROUGH Sa is firmly linked with the Mercian St. Milburga (7th century), this lady having founded the early monastery at Much Wenlock. Stoke itself was *Godestoch* in DB, apparently 'God's place', and *Stoke St. Milburg* in 1291. On one occasion St. Milburga made the waters of the River Corve rise miraculously; and there are probably pagan overtones in the fact that she was also said to be the 'protectress' of birds and crops.

St. Alkmund or St. Ealhmund (early 9th century) is also a well-known name in Shropshire. The name itself, which literally means 'Guardian of the heathen temple', OE *ealh* plus *mund,* occurs in ALCASTON Sa (*Aelmundestune* DB), ALKINGTON Sa, Gl, ELMSTONE HARDWICKE Gl, and ALMINGTON St. However, it is not an uncommon name, and - as with the names borne by moneyers - the author cannot claim that, when it occurs in a given place name, it refers to any particular Ealhmund or Alkmund. The saint himself was buried in Shropshire, but his remains were later removed to Derby.

ATTINGHAM Sa (*Atingeham* DB), which has become ATCHAM, has a church dedicated to St. Eata (7th century) of Hexham - though again, there is some doubt as to whether the settlement-name is directly connected with the saint. What cannot be doubted is that the Church frequently turned names of this type to advantage - even, on occasions, 'planting' relics which were later conveniently 'discovered' and then displayed. Meanwhile the name Eata is also found in ETLOE Gl, 'Eata's mound' - which, on the face of it, has a pagan flavour.

A similar pagan flavour is detectable in the personal name Wīgstān, literally 'Idol-stone' - OE *wīg-stān,* though in most cases, of course, the original meanings of names like this would tend to be gradually forgotten. The 8th-century St. Wīgstān of Mercia (also recorded as St. Wīstān) is assumed to be commemorated by WISTANSTOW Sa, WISTANSWICK Sa and WISTESTON He (*Wystaneston* 1198). The first place-name here means 'Wīgstān's holy place' - OE *stōw* could have this sense - and the saint is said to have been murdered here by his uncle for political reasons; the other two are ordinary settlement names. Another saint who met a violent end, Oswald of Northumbria, gave his name to OSWESTRY Sa (*Oswaldestre* 1272), probably 'Oswald's cross', which is near the scene of his death in battle. (Oswestry was recorded as *Blancmuster,* i.e. 'White minster', in 1233). Here, too, the connexion between the place-name and the saint may be due to wisdom - or opportunism - after the event.

Yet another personal name with pagan overtones is Ealhburg or Alburga, which could mean 'Idol fort'. This name belonged to a West Saxon lady-saint of the early 9th century, and is found in ALPRAHAM Chs (*Alburgham* DB) and possibly in ALBERBURY Sa. Eadberht or Eadbeorht was a male saint of the 7th century; the name itself occurs in ALBRIGHT HUSSY Sa, ALBRIGHTLEE Sa, ALBRIGHTON Sa near Shrewsbury (for which we find *Adbrichton Monachorum,* 'of the monks', in 1255), ABBERTON Wo and EBRINGTON Gl. WARBURTON Chs (*Werburgtuna* c. 1150) may record the name of the 8th-century St. Werburga, KEMERTON Gl (*Cyneburgingctun* 840) that of St. Cyneburga, and ADFORTON Sa that of St. Eadfrid, 10th century. Finally, the Welsh St. Cadog may appear in the English-looking CATSLEY Sa (*Catekesle* 1255).

CRESSAGE Sa (*Cristesache* DB), 'Christ's oak', could represent a Christian re-naming of a formerly pagan spot; equally, it could record the straightforward memory of early Christian preaching. EIMSTREY Sa (*Eiminstre* DB), which contains OE *mynster,* 'monastery', points to a Christian foundation, and the same OE word explains LEOMINSTER He - which, in fact, is a translation of W. *Llanllieni,* 'Church on the streams'. HINSTOCK Sa contains OE *hīwan,* 'members of a religious house'.

As has been stated, the stories of saints' lives often include material which obviously pre-dates Christianity, and dragons are not overlooked in this connexion. As *Beowulf* and other OE literature make clear, the barrow-guarding dragon (OE *draca*) was well established in Anglo-Saxon mythology - hence names such as DRAKELOW Wo, 'Dragon mound'. However, the constellation Draco, 'The Dragon', seen in Classical lore as guarding the apples of the Hesperides, was certainly known to Chaucer - who calls it the *Dragoun* - and the Anglo-Saxons may simply have picked up and adapted this ancient tradition. It was thought, too, that dragons inhabited and poisoned wells, and the latter were sometimes dedicated to saints reputed to have slain such monsters during their lives. St. Margaret, whose name was used to form CLEE ST. MARGARET Sa was one such saint; and there was a ST. MARGARET'S WELL near Wellington in Shropshire, so named for the reason just given. The naming of wells and springs after St. George and St. Michael is always likely to stem from the fact that they, too, slew dragons.

Fortunately, perhaps, dragons have joined the ranks of extinct creatures; and, after so many centuries during which our calendar (itself, in fact, a reformed relic of pagan times) has been marked by Christian festivals, it is hard for us to imagine a time when every Anglo-Saxon man and woman belonged to *hǣđen-cynn,* 'heathen kind'. Yet vestiges of the old beliefs linger on, as when a sneeze is greeted by a spontaneous 'Bless you' (one wonders how St. Eligius might react to that). And as we have seen in the present chapter, a single place name may mark several stages in religious progress. Yet again, the map has its own story to tell.

CHAPTER 7

FIELD NAMES

> 'Notwithstanding the land shall be divided by lot: according to the names of the tribes of their fathers they shall inherit.' - Numbers 26[55]
>
> 'Men shall buy fields for money, and subscribe evidences, and seal them, and take witnesses...' - Jeremiah 32[44]

Field names have a twofold interest. First, they reproduce in miniature the patterns already observed in place names - making statements about topography, flora, fauna, occupations, activities, customs, beliefs, superstitions, and so on. Secondly, they help us to trace some of the main threads of English agrarian history through more than a thousand years.

It is no accident that these names are arranged by parishes. From the 7th century onwards, the boundaries of the village, township or manor, with its 'head-dwelling' (OE *hēafod-bōtl*), were effectively the same as those allocated to the 'field-church' *(feld-cirice)* whose priest, following the conversions, would often be installed by lay patronage. Just as the lord claimed his dues and services, so the priest claimed his church-scot, soul-scot and tithes-in-kind. Between them these two held together the fabric of rural society.

Around the nucleus of the village with its church stretched the large, unenclosed fields (OE *feld*) upon which the local economy depended. The arable fields, usually two or three in number, were divided into furlongs, shots or flats, which were further divided into strips. In theory at least, each strip was 220 yards in length - i.e. a furlong - and 22 yards wide, giving an area of one acre. The strips as a whole were allocated not in blocks but on a lottery system, thus ensuring that good soils and less good soils were shared with an acceptable degree of fairness. Only wheat, rye, barley, oats and beans were sown, and in every year one field was left fallow. Even the meadow (OE *mǣd*) was arranged in strips (each man harvesting his own hay), so that a great deal of the land was literally 'striped' or 'streaked'; and it may be significant that in both the Germanic and the Celtic languages certain words for *strip, stripe* and *streak* tend to be interchangeable.

When we look at the fields today, invariably hedged or fenced and often of moderate size, it can be seen that the word *field* itself has undergone a considerable change of meaning. Indeed, it may be wondered how the present patchwork of enclosed fields came about. In general terms, the answer is that the old system was not flexible enough to cope with changing social and economic needs. From around 1250 at the latest right up to the 19th century, increasing numbers of copyholders - 'customary tenants' - were dispossessed or suffered loss. More and more strips passed into fewer and fewer hands through annexation, purchase, leasing or exchange; once acquired, they were consolidated for the sake of efficiency and surrounded by hedges (OE *hege, gehaeg;* W. *cae*).

Maps showing the names of fields in their newly-arranged patterns date from two different periods. From the early 18th century onwards, commissioners of enclosure began visiting individual parishes in order to deal with claims and counter-claims arising out of enclosure projects themselves. On each occasion it was ordered that field-plans should be drawn up and one copy placed in the parish chest. (The civil importance of parishes had increased as a result of Elizabeth I's Poor Laws, since it was through the former that the laws were administered). In 1836, following the Tithe Commutation Act by which tithes-in-kind were replaced by money payments, it was the turn of the tithe commissioners to visit individual parishes, and between 1836 and about 1850 fresh sets of maps were prepared on a similar basis. It is the enclosure and tithe maps, together with old estate maps, which provide most of the graphic material for field-name work.

This brief outline, however inadequate, may help to put the subject into historical perspective. As for the names dealt with in the present chapter, the vast majority belong to Shropshire parishes; however, they afford a good cross-section of the types of names encountered in England as a whole - besides providing further examples of that interplay between English and Welsh which is often as instructive as it is amusing.

Names showing OE *furlang* include FURLONG and LITTLE FURLONG (Eaton-under-Heywood). BEGGARS FURLONG (Shrewsbury St. Chad) may express a sour opinion of a soil-type or of a re-allocation resulting from an enclosure project; very similar is SORROW FURLONG (Norbury). NEAR SHUT FURLONG (Stirchley), probably containing OE *sceat,* 'shot', would have been near the village or some individual homestead - in direct contrast to OUTSTREAKS (Highley), which may record OE *strica,* Middle English *streke,* 'strip'. Middle English *flat* is represented by FLATT PIECE (Neen Sollars) and THE FLATTS (Sutton Maddock). THE SHRIVES (Westbury), from

OE *scrīfan,* 'to allot' or OE *gescrīf,* 'judgment', could represent either an original allocation of land by lot* or a re-adjustment at a later date. COPYHOLD MEADOW (Claverley) and FREEHOLDERS WOOD (Westbury) are perfect examples of names describing ancient types of tenure. SEVERAL MEADOW (Crudgington) would have been held 'in severalty', or privately. RHANDIR (Oswestry) is Welsh, literally 'Share-land', as is ERROW GAM (Selattyn), 'Crooked acre'.

Statements about the lie of the land are plentiful, as are statements regarding field shapes and sizes, types of crop, quality and colour of soil, and so on. As with place names, however, there is often a deceptive overlap between what appear to be straightforward references to flora and fauna and the activities with which these were connected; examples of this overlap will be given later on.

Meanwhile HANGING FURLONG (Pontesbury) was on a hillside (OE *hangende*), while NETHERLANDS (OE *neođera,* 'lower') in Bedstone was not. Welsh influence is seen in MAES CYMERY (Melverley), which lay near the confluence (W. *cymer*) of the Severn and the Vyrnwy. BYTHAM (Ercall Magna) is OE *bytme,* 'valley', 'hollow'. TRUMLEY (Waters Upton) may contain W. *trum,* 'ridge', while CAE BONK (Oswestry) is W. *cae,* 'field' combined with the well-known Shropshire *bank,* 'slope'. A streamlet or gully (OE *sīc*) determined the naming of BROOMSITCH MEADOW and SMALL SITCH (Richards Castle); while THE SMETHENS (Burford) and GWASTAD (Clun) indicate level land (OE *smethe,* W. *gwastad,* both meaning 'level'). BEDGLEY (Rodington) was in the bend of a river, OE *becge.*

The BIG PIECE, BIG MEADOW, GREAT FAR TILLAGE, LITTLE ORCHARD and LITTLE MEADOW of Neen Sollars are paralleled by similar descriptions of size in many other parishes. Rather less obvious is MICKLE LEASOW (Wistanstow), from OE *micel,* 'great' and *lǣs/lǣswe,* 'pasture'. THE HIDE (Shrewsbury St. Mary) records OE *hīd,* the ancient measure of land - anywhere between 40 and 120 acres - taken as sufficient to support a single family. THE GORES (Berrington) is from OE *gār,* 'spear(head)', and refers to wedge-shaped pieces of land left over from the original open field lay-outs. NETCHELLS (Alberbury) shows incorrect word-division of OE *ān(e) ecels,* 'an addition', of the same type as we saw with NASH Sa in Chapter 3. SEVEN RUDGES (Clee St. Margaret) retains the

* The place name SHRIVENHAM Brk (*Scrivenham* 821) presents an interesting parallel. Cp. also COELBREN Pow (Chapter 6).

earlier West Midland pronunciation of OE *hrycg,* 'ridge'; the reference may be to medieval ridge-and-furrow ploughing, but we also find FAR SEVEN RUDGES MEADOW (Neenton). The form of DDOL MEADOW (Fitz) points to W. *dôl,* 'meadow', as the source, initial *d* having changed to *dd* after a (lost) definite article (W. *dôl* is sometimes difficult to distinguish from English *dole,* 'share'). CAE CAM (Oswestry) is certainly Welsh and means 'Crooked field'. HAIR MEADOW (Hyssington) shows corruption of W. *hir,* 'long', while ACKILANDS (Shaw) could derive either from OE *aecer,* 'acre' or from W. *achul,* 'narrow'.

Already, then, we see how Borderlands field names faithfully reflect the ease with which English and Welsh interact with each other in this area, tending to become confused or conflated. It is possible that a classic case of confusion is provided by CAE HOSEN (St. Martin's); this means 'Stocking field' - but in a sense quite different from that of STOCKINGS (Worthen) and the STOCKING FIELD found elsewhere, which derive from OE *stocc,* 'tree-stump' and refer to lands where trees have been felled. The Welsh name contains W. *hosan,* a quite unconnected word denoting the other kind of stocking, i.e. the kind worn on the leg! Whether CAE HOSEN represents a misguided adaptation of the English 'stocking' names, or whether real hosiers plied their trade in this particular field, the author unfortunately cannot say.

Names referring to crops include RYEGRASS PIECE (Neenton), RYE MOORS, BIG RYE MOORS and LITTLE RYE MOORS (all Eaton-under-Heywood), and BARLEY FIELD (Shrewsbury Holy Cross and St. Giles) - all of which speak for themselves. BEN FURLONG (West Felton) is explained by the Middle English *bene,* 'bean', WHAT FURLONG (Albrighton) by OE *hwǣt,* 'wheat', and BEAR CROFT (Hinstock) by OE *bere,* 'barley', while W. *barlys,* 'barley' may account for the 16th-century form BARLEISFELDE (Diddlebury). In general, however, field names referring to the old staple crops are not especially numerous - a fact due in part, perhaps, to the new uses to which the enclosed fields were put. (At one time, for example, the HOPYARD LEASOW of Neenton was presumably pastureland, OE *lǣswe;* and names of this 'mixed' type are far from uncommon). If MILLIONS MEADOW (Rushbury) is not a 'mocking' name - stemming from its small size - it may contain W. *meillion,* 'clover'; the practice of sowing clover in order to improve soils began in the 17th century.

Soil-types themselves often receive specific mention. Thus we find BIG and LITTLE LIMESTONE LEASOW (Neenton); Richards Castle has CLAYHILL and CLAYHILL FIELD, while its PUDDING BAG HILL - indicating soggy ground - is echoed by the CLAY PUDDINGS of Prees and the OOZE HILL of Withington. Loam (OE *lām*) explains LAMPITS (Shrewsbury St. Mary), and the marl of MARLPIT FIELD (Richards Castle) recalls the ancient MARGIDUNUM ('Marly fort') mentioned in Chapter 3, though the former name refers to the deliberate practice of soil-marling. THE VAUGHNOG (West Felton), from W. *mawnog,* 'peat bog' is interesting in that the initial *m* has here changed to *v* after the definite article; this change is normal in Cornish and Breton, much less so in Welsh, where we should expect *fawnog* - and FOWNOG does in fact occur with the same meaning of 'peat bog'. It is possible that direct Cornish influence is behind FURTHER HADDLEMASS (Shrewsbury St. Mary); for it appears that the word *attle* - used by the old Stiperstones miners to denote slag - corresponds to Corn. *atal,* 'mine-waste'. SANDHILL MEADOW (Eaton-under-Heywood) seems self-explanatory, while STANLEY MEADOW (Stoke St. Milborough), from OE *stān,* 'stone' is parelleled by CLOUD (Berrington), showing the rare OE *clūd,* 'rock'. Greete has BIG and LITTLE GRITLEY and GRAVEL PIT MEADOW, as well as THE FINDINGS; this latter field was next to a smithy, and may record the presence of iron ores.

Activities and occupations feature just as strongly in field names as they did in the place names discussed in Chapter 4. In addition (as noted above) various field names which at first glance seem to make simple statements about local flora and fauna, or to be purely topographical, are found to have wider significance - and here the comparison is with Chapter 3.

Falling into this second category are - among others - RUSHY MEADOW (frequent), indicating fields where rushes (OE *rysc*) would have been grown for the making of both rush lights and baskets; HOLLY LEASOW (Myndtown), HOLLINSDALE (Ercall Magna) and CAE HOLLINS (Ellesmere) - 'Holly field' - whose holly (OE *holegn,* dialectal *hollin*) was used for winter fodder (these names are echoed in Selattyn by NANT KELYN DUON, 'Brook of the black holly'); BUTTON PIECE (Mainstone), the first word here probably denoting the teasel used in fulling; WIMBERRIES (Wistanstow) and WINBERRY HILL (Ruyton-XI-Towns), both showing OE *wīn-berige,* literally 'wine-berry' and denoting the bilberry or whortleberry - cp. BILBERRY HILL (Shifnal) - from which wine must have been made; PIGEON CLOSE (Neen Savage), recording the fact that this bird was an important food-fource and echoed by various names in other parishes, including CULVERHOUSE CROFT (Shrewsbury St. Chad), from OE *culfre,* 'dove', 'pigeon'; and BUCKSTONE (Church Stretton), which - like BUXTON (Stoke upon Tern) - refers not to the animal but to a large stone called a bucking stone on which linen was washed quarterly.

Nor should we forget the culinary and medicinal use of flowers and herbs. KITCHEN MEADOW (Billingsley), PEPPER HOLE (Westbury) - peppermint, though pepper itself (OE *pipor*) was known - and GARLICK CROFT (Shrewsbury St. Mary) point to the culinary side, while POPE FURLONG (Munslow) - poppies, OE *popig* - may indicate the preparation of opium (cp. DRUGMAN'S HILL in Bridgnorth St. Leonard), since OE *papig-drenc,* 'poppy-drink' occurs. FOXGLOVES (Alberbury) could likewise refer to the use of digitalis; certainly white clover (cp. the place name CLAVERLEY Sa) was pressed into service as the chief ingredient of a drink supposed to heal sores, and the OE *Leechdoms* tell us that the bark of quickbeam, elder, willow, sallow, wych-elm, oak, birch, dogwood and myrtle, as well as broom, nettles, centaury, catkins, bog-myrtle, ivy, tansy, docks, lichens, betony, mallows, agrimony, burdock, rue, viper's bugloss, dill, pennyroyal and various other plants, were all used in the making of 'salves' (radishes, somewhat ungallantly, are specially recommended as an antidote against the chatter of women!). Again, then, we see that the natural environment was diligently exploited - and of course, field names such as DOCK YARD (Condover), GAUL (Richards Castle), from OE *gagel, 'bog-myrtle',* HARDHEAD PIECE (Lydham) - centaury - and ORGAN HILL (Wroxeter) - pennyroyal or marjoram, from the Latin *origanum* - may all point to deliberate cultivation.

This was indeed the case where dye-yielding plants were concerned; and these are convenient items with which to begin our review of names linked to activities and occupations proper. GAUDY GROUND (Pontesbury) is from French *gaude,* 'dyer's weed'; this gave a yellow dye and may possibly by compared with YELLOW MEADOW (Kinnerley); THE WADLANDS (Moreton Corbet) records OE *wād,* 'woad', while a 'woad-man' owned WODEMANSEY (Shrewsbury St. Mary); Condover has SAFFRON BUTTS (the word *saffron* is a borrowing from Arabic *za'faran),* Shrewsbury St. Chad has LE MADERYORDE, showing OE *maedere,* 'madder', while the DYEHOUSE PIECE of Oldbury and the DYER LEASOW of Ruyton-XI-Towns show how the land was put to industrial or craft uses. (As was mentioned in an earlier chapter, dye, OE *dēag,* was well known to the Anglo-Saxons).

The range of other activities and occupations recorded is considerable; and while, of course, a fair number of the names listed below may date from the post-medieval period, Old and Middle English vocabulary - not to mention Welsh - make it equally clear that many of the activities and occupations themselves were known and/or practised long before (this, it is to be hoped, was brought out in Chapter 4).

Between them, Richards Castle, Ashford Bowdler and Ashford Carbonel have - among other names of similar type - MILL MEADOW, MILL CROFT and UPPER and LOWER MILSTONE (probably OE *mylen-stān,* 'millstone', rather than 'milestone', OE *mīl-gemet*); UPPER and LOWER WHETTER (whetstones); GRAVEL PIT, UPPER and LOWER GRAVEL PIT FIELD, QUARRY CROFT ORCHARD and THE QUARRY PIECE; COLLEY CROFT, which could refer to coal or charcoal, and COLLICOTT MOOR (same); WRIGHT'S CLOSE (OE *wyrhta,* 'wright', 'craftsman'); COOPER'S ORCHARD, a cooper of course being a cask-maker; TANNER'S GROUND; CARTER'S FIELD, where carts may have been made; and BUTCHER'S MEADOW, either belonging to a butcher or site of a slaughter-house.

Bitterley shows LIMEKILN MEADOW and LIMEKILN LEASOW, as well as KILN LEASOW, where bricks or tiles may have been made, and COLLEY PIT. In Worthen are BRICKKILN FIELD and UPPER and LOWER BRICKYARD; BAKEHOUSE BANK; BIG and LITTLE MILLSTONE; WALK MILL MEADOW (fulling); MALTHOUSE LEASOW; MILLERS MEADOW; SINKWELL PIECE; SKINLEY - possibly indicating the treatment of skins. Neen Sollars extends the list with POTTERS LEASOW and CLAYPITS - these two may have had a direct connexion with each other - while the COTHER CROFT of Milson probably records dialectal *cather,* 'hemp' (cp. W. *carth* - same meaning - and CARTHER RIDDING, Whitchurch). Eaton-under-Heywood contributes CHAPMANS HEATH and CHAPMANS MEADOW (trading); MILL MEADOW; LIMEKILN GROUND and LIMEKILN PIECE; SPELLERS MEADOW, where speeches - OE *spell* - were made; SAWPIT MEADOW (OE *sagu,* 'saw'). Neenton has QUARRY LEASOW next to LIMEKILN LEASOW; MILL LAYS; and the HOPYARD LEASOW here, like similar names elsewhere, is itself evidence of brewing.

To go on repeating the same or near-identical names would be tedious, but permutations of the above forms are scattered liberally throughout the Shropshire parishes. Nor is there any lack of other interesting information. BICKERIDGE (Hinstock) echoes the Cheshire place name BICKERTON and indicates the presence of bee-keepers, OE *beocere.* TENTERS (Cheswardine) recalls earlier remarks about TINTERN Gw, and we also find FRAME YARD (Kenley); both names refer to cloth-stretching. THE WHITENING JACKS (Westbury), OE *hwītian,* which was open ground on which linen was bleached, may be compared with the *Blechelie* mentioned in Shropshire DB, Middle English *blechen,* 'to bleach'. OIL ROCK MEADOW in Pitchford presumably refers to the pitch or bitumen of this area (Chapter 3). Tiles, OE *tigel,* were either made or dug up in TILE PITS (Tugford). WANHAM (Shrewsbury High Cross and St. Giles) is from OE *waegn,* 'wagon', 'cart' and may be a variation on CARTER'S FIELD, above. BARGE GUTTER (Shrewsbury St. Chad) was a special channel cut in the Severn to facilitate the passage of river traffic, while HORSE BOAT FIELDS (Shrewsbury St. Mary) tells of the pulling of river craft by horses. Traffic on land is interestingly attested by the LITTLE LONDON of Oswestry and elsewhere, for fields so named were reserved for cattle drovers on their way to London; many of these drovers came from Wales, and in Dyfed we find an equivalent Welsh place name, LLUNDAIN-FACH, 'Little London', near Nancwnlle. (Cp. also UCKINGTON Sa, mentioned in Chapter 4). We even find a LEPERS ACRE (Burford); and again, it is not impossible that CLAVERTON Chs (*Claventone* DB) was originally from W. *cleifion,* plural of *claf,* 'leper', 'sick person'. There are also USURER'S MEADOW in Shrewsbury St. Chad (see Chapter 4), MALTMAN'S YARD (Cound), MERCHANTS MEADOW (Baschurch), TINMAN'S LEASOW (Melverley) - a tinman was a tin-smith or a tin-dealer - and SHOEMAKERS CROFT (Shrewsbury St. Mary).

A few further remarks on 'hybrids' and confused forms will not be out of place, since it seems certain that there is a rich harvest still to be reaped in this particular field.

CAE CIL BRICK (Llanyblodwel) appears to be straightforward Welsh adaptation of English 'brick-kiln', since W. *cyl* means 'kiln'; the meaning is thus 'Enclosure of the brick-kiln'. BABYTREE LAND (Edgton), earlier *Babetrevorlonge,* could be explained by Br. *babu,* 'white-heart cherry (tree)'; Breton influence in the Midlands following the Conquest was not negligible. OLIVE BANK (Alberbury) may be a corruption of W. *olaf,* 'last', 'hindmost'. THREE ANVILS, too, in Shrewsbury St.

Mary, could show corruption *via* local pronunciation of OE and Modern English *handful(l)s,* intended as a 'mocking' name. Meanwhile there appears to be no argument about the charming PRESTON ARGUE (Preston upon the Weald Moors), an English adaptation of W. *argae,* 'dam', 'embankment'.

OE *croft* was borrowed into Welsh as *crofft.* When this new word was treated as feminine, it became *(y) grofft* after the definite article; and, when this definite article was lost (as it so often was), a false new form *grofft* seems to have arisen. Treated as feminine in turn, this became *(y) rofft* after the definite article, showing normal loss of *g.* Hence, then, ROFT-Y-PISTILL (Oswestry), 'Croft of the waterfall', beside the alternative PYSTIL CROFT.

Technicalities such as this may not be to everyone's taste. Nevertheless, they do help to bring out the special fascination of names in the Borderlands, where two languages of equal vigour can be positively shown to have come into conflict - and to have made their own kind of peace - in shaping many of the forms handed down to us. (One suspects that the Domesday inquisitors, who spoke in French and wrote in Latin, needed to keep all their wits about them in dealing with this awkward area).

It remains only to point out that open-field farming was never the norm in Wales. Thus W. *cae,* whose primary meaning is 'hedge', came very early on to denote the land hedged in, i.e. a field; the transfer of meaning reflects ancient practice. In England, however, where OE *hege,* Middle English *hegge* (which, like OE *gehaeg,* Middle English *hay,* also means 'hedge') might have been expected to develop exactly the same sense as *cae,* the development has failed to take place. It is OE *feld,* 'open land', which has prevailed - weathering all historical change and its effects upon topography.

CHAPTER 8

SOME UNSOLVED NAMES

Further Notes on THE BERTH (Chapter 2)
The first thing to note is that there are at least 100 place names in England which contain the English word *thorn* as an element. Some of these names refer to places fortified by thorn-hedges (e.g. THORNBURY He, Gl, THORNBROUGH Nb, YW), others are connected with prehistoric sites of one sort or another (e.g. THICKTHORN Do, where there are two long barrows). That hedges were used as a means of protection in early England is shown by an entry for 547 in the *Anglo-Saxon Chronicle,* which states that Bamborough in Northumberland, 'Bebba's fort', was 'fenced in first with a hedge *(hegge)* and afterwards with a wall'.

W. *perthgae* means 'quickset hedge' (*perth* plus *cae*). In the *Gallic War,* Caesar tells us that at least one tribe in Gaul used branches intertwined with briers and thorns *(rubis sentibusque)* for the purposes of defence. Thus the place name SPINIS (Berkshire), 'At the thorns', recorded from Romano-Celtic Britain, makes very good sense when looked at in this sort of context.

Place names in Wales and the Welsh Borderlands containing W. *perth* (plural *perthi*), 'thornbush', 'thicket' include PERTHI (Sa), PERTHILLWYDION in Clwyd, 'Grey thornbushes', TŶ'N-Y-BERTH Pow, 'House in the thornbush', CRAIG BERTH-LWYD in Glamorgan, 'Rock of the grey thornbush', BERTH-DDU Pow, 'Black thornbush', LLWYN-Y-BERTH in Anglesey, 'Grove of the thornbush', and many others. CASTELL DRAENEN in Dyfed contains W. *draenen,* 'thorn' and means 'Thorn stronghold'.

In view of names such as THE VAUGHNOG (from *mawnog,* Chapter 7) and many others dealt with throughout this book, it seems very probable that THE BERTH Sa, St signifies 'The thornbush' and is not connected with OE *burg,* 'fort' (which, in the Borderlands, sometimes led to the form *burf*). Since W. *perth* is generally much less likely than OE *burh* to imply the existence of an earthwork or tumulus as such, the derivation from the Welsh word of BERTH HILL (on the Worcestershire-Gloucestershire border) and BERTH HOUSE Sa (near Shelve), where there are no forts, is not inconsistent with the derivation from the same word of THE BERTH Sa (near Baschurch), which happens to be a fort. This site, like THE BERTH St, is surrounded by a bank and ditch, and thorn-hedges may once have existed at both these places.

Further Notes on CRŪC/CRUG and CROSS

Old Welsh *crūc,* later *crug,* 'hill(ock)' (Chapter 2) was borrowed into OE as *crūc.* This borrowed word was later pronounced *crüc(h)* or *cric(h),* and a good case has been made out for the derivation of some CRUCK-, CRU(T)CH-, CROOK-, CRICK-, CRICH-, CREEK- and CREECH- place names in terms of the original Old Welsh word.

However, caution is still needed, particularly where CROOK-, CRUCK- and CRU(T)CH- names are concerned. The reason is that there was another OE word *crūc,* which meant 'cross'. This word, derived from Latin *crux/crucis,* existed alongside OE *cros,* a borrowing of Old Norse *kross* (itself a borrowing of Old Irish *cros*). In Middle English it became *crucche* or *crouche,* and a 'Crutched' or 'Crouched' Friar was one who wore a habit emblazoned with a cross. The frequent use of crosses as landmarks on hills (e.g. CROSSENS La, 'Headland with crosses') as well as in valleys (e.g. CROSSDALE Cu, 'Valley with crosses') indicates that OE *crūc,* 'cross' ought not to be ignored in place names as a possible alternative to the OE *crūc,* 'hill(ock)' borrowed from Old Welsh.

CRUCKMEOLE Sa (*Meole* 1327) is a CRUCK- name making good sense in terms of the latter word if we see it as *crūc,* 'hill(ock)' plus W. *moel,* 'bare' - with *moel* having come (through misunderstanding) to be applied to the river MEOLE. Nearby CRUCKTON Sa, on the other hand, was *Crocton* in 1272, *Crokton* in 1308, and seems more likely to contain W. *crog* - which, in fact, means 'cross' - than *crūc,* 'hill(ock)'. CRUTCH Wo (*Cruchia* 1285) - not least on account of its modern pronunciation - seems to point to OE *crūc,* 'cross' as the source. CHURCHILL Wo (near Kidderminster) is not on a hill(ock) but in a valley; here, it is not impossible that OE *crūc,* 'cross' was confused with OE *cyrc,* 'church'; topographically speaking, the *hill* element (OE *hyll,* Middle English *hul*) presents a problem.

CROOKBARROW HILL Wo (*Cruchulle* 1182) looks like a natural candidate for explanation in terms of W. *crūc.* However, the form *Crokberewe,* c. 1225, may indicate that the original first element was W. *crog* in the sense 'gibbet', 'gallows' (Br. *kroug,* Corn. *crōk*).

CRUCKTON Sa, CRUTCH Wo and CHURCHILL Wo would appear to the author to be unsolved, or at least lacking satisfactory explanations; while CROOKBARROW HILL Wo might repay further investigation. And one further point remains to be made. If W. *crūc/crug,* 'hill(ock)' is accepted as explaining certain types of place names in England, how many other Celtic elements, borrowed or corrupted, may lie unrecognised in the mass of early forms available to us? This question, which was posed by Professor W. G. Hoskins more than 20 years ago, is still largely untackled.

SELECT BIBLIOGRAPHY

Adkins, Lesley and Roy *Handbook of British Archaeology* (London, 1982)

Anderson, J. C. *Shropshire: Early History and Antiquities* (London, 1864)

Baring-Gould, S. *Lives of the Saints* (16 vols) (London, 1897-8)

Bowcock, E. W. *Shropshire Place Names* (Shrewsbury, 1923)

Brooke, G. C. *English Coins* (London, 1950)

Burne, C. S. (ed.) *Shropshire Folk-Lore* (London, 1883)

Cameron, K. *English Place-Names* (London, 1961)

Darby, H. C. and Terrett, I. B. (ed.) *The Domesday Geography of Midland England* (Cambridge, 1971)

Davies, E. (ed.) *A Gazetteer of Welsh Place-Names* (Cardiff, 1957)

Dodgshon, R. A. *The Origin of British Field Systems* (London, 1980)

Dyer, J. *The Penguin Guide to Prehistoric England and Wales* (London, 1982)

Finn, R. W. *Domesday Book: A Guide* (London, 1973)

Foxall, H. D. G. *Shropshire Field-Names* (Shrewsbury, 1980)

Frere, S. *Britannia* (London, 1974)

Galbraith and Tait (ed.) *Herefordshire Domesday* (Balliol College MS) (London, 1950)

Gelling, M. *Signposts to the Past* (London, 1988)

Grinsell, L. V. *Folklore of Prehistoric Sites in Britain* (London, 1976)

Hodgson, J. M. *Soils of the Ludlow District* (London, 1972)

Hoskins, W. G. *Fieldwork in Local History* (London, 1967)

Houlder, C. *Wales: An Archaeological Guide* (London, 1978)

Jones, J. M. *A Welsh Grammar* (Oxford, 1913)

Levett, A. E. *Studies in Manorial History* (Oxford, 1938)

Millward, R. and Robinson, A. *The Welsh Marches* (London, 1971)

Nicholl, H. G. *Forest of Dean* (London, 1858)

Pierce, G. O. *The Place-Names of Dinas Powys Hundred* (Cardiff, 1968)

Plummer, C. and Earle, J. (ed.) *The Anglo-Saxon Chronicle* (Oxford, 1892)

Plymley, J. *General View of the Agriculture of Shropshire* (London, 1813)

Rees, W. *South Wales and The March 1284-1415* (Oxford, 1924)

Richards, W. *English-Welsh Dictionary* (Bristol, 1759) (Welsh-English companion volume, Carmarthen, 1823)

Smith, A. H. *English Place-name Elements* (Cambridge, 1956)

Stenton, F. M. *Anglo-Saxon England* (Oxford, 1943)

Thorpe, L. (trans.) Gerald of Wales: *The Journey Through Wales and The Description of Wales* (London, 1980)
Toller, T. N. *An Anglo-Saxon Dictionary* (based on J. Bosworth) (Oxford, 1898)
Trépos, P. *Grammaire Bretonne* (Rennes, 1980)

INDEX

(Additional Abbreviations:- An = Anglesey; Cl = Clwyd; Dyf = Dyfed; Gla = Glamorgan; Gwy = Gwynedd. Lost settlements, field names and street names are in italics.)